WEIRD WISDOM FOR THE SECOND HALF OF LIFE

A Book for Men (and those who value them)

By James Hazelwood

© 2023

Ours is an age that is desperately in need of guides of the inner world. This lovely offering from James Hazelwood seeks to address just this need. With warmth and wit, Hazelwood reminds us that, not only does life continue after midlife, in some crucial ways it really begins. This book is both an invitation and an initiation into the meaning to be found in the second half of life. It is a tour of the often-unexpected places where wisdom can be found during this time taken with a compassionate and trustworthy guide.

~ Jason E. Smith, Jungian Analyst, author of *Religious but Not Religious: Living a Symbolic Life*, and creator of the *Digital Jung* podcast.

Chapter after chapter in Weird Wisdom, James Hazelwood articulates questions on the page that many hearts carry quietly and alone. Let these pages be your invitation to go willingly and deeply into becoming a wisened elder. With this book as your guide, you can approach the threshold into wonder, enchantment, and the liberating mother tongue of metaphor, and maybe even find yourself at home there.

~ Jennie Isbell Shinn, M.Div., LMT, Spiritual Director and Dreamworker.

Weird Wisdom for the Second Half of Life
A Book for Men (and those who value them)

Copyright © 2023 by James Hazelwood. All rights reserved.

No part of this publication may be reproduced, distributed or transmitted in any form or by any means, including photocopying, recording, or other electronic or mechanical methods, without the prior written permission of the publisher, except in the case of brief quotations embodied in critical reviews and certain other noncommercial uses permitted by copyright law.

Although the author and publisher have made every effort to ensure that the information in this book was correct at press time, the author and publisher do not assume and hereby disclaim any liability to any party for any loss, damage, or disruption caused by errors or omissions, whether such errors or omissions result from negligence, accident, or any other cause.

Adherence to all applicable laws and regulations, including international, federal, state and local governing professional licensing, business practices, advertising, and all other aspects of doing business in the U.S., Canada or any other jurisdiction is the sole responsibility of the reader and consumer.

Neither the author nor the publisher assumes any responsibility or liability whatsoever on behalf of the consumer or reader of this material. Any perceived slight of any individual or organization is purely unintentional.

The resources in this book are provided for informational purposes only and should not be used to replace the specialized training and professional judgment of a health care or mental health care professional.

Neither the author nor the publisher can be held responsible for the use of the information provided within this book. Please always consult a trained professional before making any decision regarding treatment of yourself or others.

Unless otherwise noted, all Scripture quotations are from the New Revised Standard Version, Anglicized Edition. Copyright © 1989, 1995 by the Division of Christian Education of the National Council of the Churches of Christ in the U.S.A.
Scripture quotations marked The Message are taken from The Message. Copyright © by Eugene H. Peterson, 1993, 1994, 1995, 1996, 2000, 2001, 2002, NavPress Publishing Group.

ISBN: 978-1-7333886-2-7
Credits
Copy editors: Janna Eversmeyer   ej3906@gmail.com

Table of Contents

Preface v
Introduction vii
Section One 1
Chapter 1   Seeking Wisdom at this Stage of Life 1
Chapter 2   In Search of Wisdom 21
Poetry Interlude: On the Turning of my 63rd Year 29
Section Two 31
Chapter 3   Wonder 31
Chapter 4   Enchantment 45
Chapter 5   Integrity 65
Chapter 6   Relationships 79
Chapter 7   Destiny 91
Epilogue   Dreams as Windows into Weird Wisdom 103
References 119
Acknowledgements 127

Preface

This book needed a subtitle. But the marketing department opposed the idea. Nevertheless, I've added it. This is "a book for men and those who value them." In many ways, this is an autobiographical sketch of my path across the bridge from the first half of my life to the second half. Because I am a man, I can't help but write about my experience. While there is a lot here for women as well, and I've researched and spoken to many, it goes without saying that everything on these pages goes through a filter. That filter is this 60-plus-year-old white guy, firstborn in a family of three boys and cursed/blessed with a call to exercise leadership in the context of spirituality.

But this book is also intended to be an alternative voice in the now crowded field of books on retirement, encore careers, mid-life, and next phase of life planning. Most of those books focus on the external world of people, places, and productivity. Instead, this one asks about the inner world of mind, soul, and legacy.

The world needs both approaches.

So, for all of you scratching your head in this second half, wondering what's going on, I hope this book helps.

If you are interested in an ongoing conversation about some of the themes in this book, I invite you to check out my website, www.jameshazelwood.net. In addition, there is a monthly newsletter on many topics covered here, and you are welcome to subscribe.

Introduction

In 2007, just two years shy of my fiftieth birthday, I had the following dream during one of our service trips to a remote village in Honduras.

I have decided to enroll in a German language instruction class where professor H.S. is to be the instructor. (She is the same professor I had in waking life for my Spanish classes in preparation for this trip to Honduras.) We introduce ourselves on the final day of class, and I say that I am not very good at languages. This professor agrees with me. But I am in the class because I like to learn. We seem to be waiting for something, but no one knows who or what. Finally, the former bishop from New York arrives to much fanfare, like a head of state style welcome. His wife and two daughters accompany him. He is to preach at a worship service held at an ancient coliseum. Before the worship service, I learned that the pastor of the coliseum church was involved in a scandal of an undefined nature. The bishop decides to allow the man to work things through instead of removing him immediately. I seem pleased with his decision, and I wonder if I am that pastor. After the worship, the German/Spanish professor appears and approaches the bishop and me. She thanks the bishop and then turns to me and says, "You have a pastorate to rebuild."

I held on to this dream for a long time before discussing it with anyone. Now, some fifteen years later, I can see its meaning. Glimpses of understanding unfolded over the years. It is a quintessential dream of a man at the turning point from the first half of life toward the second half. The dreamer, namely me, is to learn new languages. A feminine character will be the instructor. A bishop, a symbol of authority and reverence, arrives accompanied by three women, forming a symbol of complete wholeness.[1] The bishop preaches at an ancient coliseum, where a scandal-ridden pastor presides. But the bishop allows the man to stay and "work things through." And the concluding line captures it all. Addressing the dreamer, the professor says, "You have a pastorate to rebuild." In other words, the turn toward the second half of life involves a new structure, a new language, and a time to rebuild the inner landscape.

I had spent my 20s, 30s, and 40s creating or building a life, a family, a career. My efforts and gifts resulted in achievements, recognition, family. Yet, in my late 40s, I began to flatten out. Our son headed off to college, and the work no longer energized me. I dabbled in hobbies and considered leaving the ministry for another career. Then, two years before this dream, my father died at 78. I now wondered how much time I had on this earth. The lyrics from the Talking Heads song *Once in a Lifetime* echoed through my mind.

> And you may find yourself behind the wheel of a large automobile
> And you may find yourself in a beautiful house, with a beautiful wife
> And you may ask yourself, "Well, how did I get here?

---

[1] Carl Jung believed that symbols had powerful connections to the unconscious as well as the historical patterns of life. A symbol involving four is one such symbol. This gathering of four people, a man and three women, is but one example of a quaternity. Jung found these symbols of quaternity to point toward wholeness. "The quaternity is one of the most widespread archetypes and has also proved to be one of the most useful schemata for representing the arrangement of the functions by which the conscious mind takes its bearings. It is like the crossed threads in the telescope of our understanding. The cross formed by the points of the quaternity is no less universal and has in addition the highest possible moral and religious significance for Western man. Similarly the circle, as the symbol of completeness and perfect being, is a widespread expression for heaven, sun, and God; it also expresses the primordial image of man and the soul." Jung, "The Psychology of the Transference," CW Vol., 16, par., 405.

I asked how I got there, where it was all going, and what does this life mean? I've spent the last fifteen years asking those and many other questions. The answers I've found are, well, they're weird. There are many different takes on this chapter of life, which we often call midlife. Most of the advice centers around losing weight, exercising more, healthy eating, encore career planning. Much of that can be helpful, and books addressing those topics have served me well. But the path through the second half of life is more than what we do externally. It also involves an internal or spiritual journey.

The late John Romig Johnson, Episcopal priest and Jungian analyst, once told me as I sat in his office, "When people hit midlife, they discover three things. One. Life is not fair. Two. They are a lot more like their parents than they wish to admit. Three. They have a soul."

Despite an early vocational calling to serve as a Lutheran pastor along with a graduate education from two theological schools, I'm not sure I realized the importance of soul work until somewhere in the middle passage of life. What I've learned through the years, and keep learning, by the way, involves some weird concepts, ideas, and stories. This book explores them through a **WEIRD** approach.

WONDER
ENCHANTMENT
INTEGRITY
RELATIONSHIPS
DESTINY

This is a book for people over 50. Sure, you can try and give it to that niece or nephew just getting out of grad school or finishing up their tour of duty in the Navy. I won't mind if you purchase more copies of this book. But that young person probably can't relate to this one. Honestly, they shouldn't relate. They are at a different stage in life. They are supposed to be building their first half-lives. So I think you are better off encouraging them and celebrating their achievements. After all, life is also about building up; let's give them the time and encouragement to do so. Career, family, success, achievement, promotions, children, and social impact are all essential aspects of maturing in our society. So, let's throw a party and honor their progress. That's all first half of life work.

But us post-50 types are likely to realize that a shift has occurred, and we might be open to some weirdness. As I enter my sixth decade, I've become aware of the growing number of books on the second half of life. They include proposals for encore careers, retirement planning, and better health and exercise. Those books provide a rich opportunity as you explore the outer landscape of life. This book is focused on the inner journey. What are the inner areas that need our attention?

Among the various tools we will use in seeking this weird wisdom, you'll find several stories. I use contemporary vignettes from people I've known, ancient myths and fairy tales, sacred stories from biblical literature as well as from other religions. I also describe my own memories, dreams, and reflections. Stories are central to our lives. We human beings are meaning-seeking creatures. Because of this, we tell stories, live stories. You could say we are story creatures. So, this book contains a variety of stories. As you read, I hope you will find your story here as well.

SECTION ONE

CHAPTER 1

Seeking Wisdom at this Stage in Life

*Midway along the journey of our life
I woke to find myself in a dark wood,
for I had wandered off from the straight path.*

-Dante Alighieri

Sam was in his early 50s when I came to know him. We've spoken on multiple occasions concerning his family life and work. "I feel stuck," he confided to me three years ago. Before moving to New England, he had worked in the Midwest. He'd been successful in work and was widely known among colleagues for his achievements. He and his wife raised four children who navigated high school and began establishing themselves in careers, interests, and future partners. Then, having achieved success in his career and launched his children into the world, Sam suddenly became bored. "I started searching for a new position all around the country, and we landed here. Honestly, I was hoping the move would shake me out of my doldrums. It didn't work."

Susan and her wife met in college when they lived across the hall in the dormitory. Following graduation, they each went their separate ways. Susan married a man and had two children but the couple separated. She reconnected with her friend from college, and through a variety of factors discovered her sexuality. "For me it was a movement of the spirit," as she told me about her life. "After Massachusetts legalized same-sex marriage in 2003, Anne and I formally began our life together." Her parents were initially reluctant to embrace Susan's identity, but gradually began to see how content she became. "For me the years after 40 have been the best years of my life. I began a new relationship, launched two children and now I'm pursuing the career I've always wanted." For Susan, the idea of a midlife crisis is almost a foreign concept. Her changes have been more evolutionary, connected with relationships as well as her body. "I don't know, maybe for women, the fact that we are always readjusting means the crisis is spread out. What I will say that's different now is I'm much more interested in questions of meaning and purpose than when I was younger."

Like many people, Sam and Susan express a theme common to people in middle adulthood. They move through life stages, resolve the various transitions of human development, achieve intimacy with a partner, and find success in their careers, only to find themselves in a dark wood, as Dante puts it. Establishing and achieving goals is the work we are called to do from adolescence through middle adulthood. Our energies in those efforts are critical to a healthy and satisfying life. But when we hit the midpoint, something shifts inside us. We hear a call to a different pattern. We begin asking new questions. It's almost as if we are in the process of being reborn.

This book is about the resources we need for a healthy and satisfying life in the second half. We'll explore the wisdom required to navigate this new life in the coming chapters. But first, let's look at what's going on and how we got here.

The idea that we move through life through a series of stages is not new. It dates to Homer's description of the life journey in the *Iliad* and the *Odyssey*, and continues through the teachings of biblical writers, Greek philosophers, and on into the mysticism of Hildegard of Bingen and Teresa of Ávila. Modern psychologists including Carl Jung, Erik and Joan Erikson, Bernice Neugarten, Nicola Slee, Lawrence Kohlberg, and Carol Gilligan all brought the concept forward into the modern era.

As our 21st century North American society experiences the benefits of a longer life span, we also realize that our priorities and interests at age 55 are different than at age 25. Modern psychological theory is a relatively new phenomenon and is undergoing constant reforms. As more and more women and persons with non-European backgrounds enter the field, it continues to grow and expand. While all these theories have their own unique approach, they share a common discovery. What follows is a broad overview of some of the foundational contributions to understanding the patterns of our lives.

Approaches to the Stages of Life

The Swiss psychologist Carl Gustav Jung and the Austrian Sigmund Freud are often described, along with Alfred Adler, as the founders of modern depth psychology. Their writings and ideas influenced much of Western culture for over one hundred years. While Freud is more well known, Jung's work has grown in importance as his concepts have made their way into modern society. Introvert, Extrovert, Persona, Complex, Archetype, Synchronicity, are all ideas that originated with Jung. Carl Jung and Sigmund Freud were central figures in the early years of psychology, but in 1913, their friendship and partnership collapsed over fundamental differences around the theory of instincts. Following this termination of collaboration, there was little dialogue between these founders' analytic descendants. The Freudians and Jungians went their separate ways.

Carl Jung understood the human psyche as reaching its zenith in the middle of life. His exploration of the subject can be found in the essay "Stages of Life.[1]" He posits the four stages and compares them to the sun's natural progression, rising in the morning, making its way across the sky with a zenith at noon. "And the descent means the reversal of

---

[1] Jung, C. G., & In Campbell, J. *The Portable Jung*, 15.

all the ideals and values that were cherished in the morning ... It is as though it should draw in its rays instead of emitting them. Light and warmth decline and are at last extinguished."[2] Jung describes the first half of life as developing, strengthening, and clarifying the culture's externally appreciated values, such as career, marriage, mortgage, and possibly children. One spends the first half of life in stages one and two building a persona, that is, "a kind of mask, designed on the one hand to make a definite impression upon others, and on the other to conceal the true nature of the individual."[3]

Jung's stages of development:
1. Childhood – An archaic stage with only hints of the beginning of logical and abstract thinking as the ego begins to form.
2. Youth & Early Years – This phase begins at puberty and continues into the mid- to late 30s. This stage includes the development of sexuality accompanied by a growing awareness and the eventual realization that carefree childhood days are gone. The chief tasks of forming a life are foundational.
3. Middle Life – Beginning in one's late 30s or early 40s, this is a phase where one's anticipation of mortality begins to affect one's attitude. A more philosophical and religious outlook is nurtured.
4. Old Age – This is a time late in life when wisdom increases and the preparation for death becomes the chief focus of one's energy.

Carl Jung has only a cursory view of the early stages of one's life. He is more invested in what happens in the second half of life. This contrasts with his former mentor Sigmund Freud and other psychoanalytic schools, who spent more energy seeking to understand childhood as

---

[2] Jung, C. G., *The Portable Jung*, 15.
[3] Jung, C. G., *Two essays on analytical psychology*, 190.

a foundational aspect in one's development. Jung may have been one of the earliest to use the term midlife (Mitte des Lebens in German), and he certainly brought attention to it in his work. The word "midlife" first appeared in the English language in 1895, and as the human life span expanded during the 20th century, more and more people got the opportunity to experience it. One wonders if the midlife crisis could have even been a reality in a time when people may only have lived into their late 20s. The advent of improved housing, safe drinking water, proper hygiene, food safety, and antibiotics has given us a longer life than previous generations. It may also have given us the midlife crisis.

German-born and later American psychologist Erik Erikson trained in the psychoanalytic tradition of Sigmund Freud and was among the first and foremost theorists to develop a comprehensive theory of human social development. If Jung initiated awareness on the two halves of life and the accompanying crisis, Erikson is known for the term "identity crisis." For Erikson, this crisis occurs not just at midlife but at each stage of human development. He postulated that at each of his eight stages (later his wife Joan added a ninth stage, elderhood, for the post-75 years of age), an individual must resolve a crisis unique to that time of development. More than either Jung or Freud, Erikson emphasized the social and cultural environment as formative for individuals. His contributions to understanding how a person grows and changes in one's interaction with society significantly contribute to our understanding of the progression of human life.

Many theorists have taken up the work of Erik and Joan Erikson. As a result, social development theory has evolved and expanded from the initial nine stages to a more broadly accepted understanding of eleven development stages.[4]

---

[4] Newman, B. M., & Newman, P. R. *Development through Life: A psychosocial approach.*

1. Prenatal
2. Infancy
3. Toddler
4. Preschool
5. Primary Schooling
6. Adolescence
7. Late Adolescence
8. Early Adulthood
9. Middle Adulthood
10. Older Adulthood
11. Elderhood

If you are interested in a more thorough examination of these stages of life, I refer you to the resources listed at the conclusion of this book. But, again, we're focused on the Middle Adult to Older Adult time frames.

The Middle Adulthood phase begins in the late 30s or early 40s and continues until approximately age 60. This stage focuses on measuring accomplishments and failures principally in career and family matters. It's almost as if we have a twofold mind during these years. On the one hand, we're contemplating what we can generate, and on the other hand, wondering if we might be stagnating. Am I producing good work, a good family, and a sound financial level? Is my life making a difference? If the answers to these questions are increasingly hostile, then a sense of stagnation can dominate one's attitude.

Let's be clear here. I'm not talking about having a bad moment or day or week; instead, I'm referring to an accumulated sense of resentment. I'm thinking about a colleague named Ethan, who worked as an engineer for a large aerospace company. In one of those patterns from a bygone era, he worked for the same company his whole life and lived in the same house for nearly thirty years. When Ethan turned 51, he traveled to a college reunion to connect with old friends. There he listened to everyone's Instagram life, a phrase that refers to the idealized social media life. We want people to think it is our real life—proven by photos of vacations, hobbies, achievements, beautiful people, and beautiful food. Ethan returned home utterly depressed. He told me, "Wow, all those people have great and interesting lives. Look at mine. It's just been boring. Even when I go on vacation, it's to the same place in the Finger Lakes region every year."

Stagnation is the feeling of not having done anything to contribute to one's life or to the lives of those around you. A sense of generativity develops as one experiences satisfaction with one's accomplishments. The tasks of middle adulthood rest upon successful resolution of internal and external conflicts. At each stage, there is a crisis, and in midlife, the tasks needing resolution concern producing, nurturing, and guiding the next generation. We wrestle with the question, "Have I generated enough in my life?" Ethan's story reminds us of some people's struggles with this question. It also reminds us not to go to high school or college reunions.

As we move into our 60s, the dominant question becomes, "What kind of life have I lived?" We reflect on the good times with gladness, the hard times with a degree of respect, and our failures with a growing sense of forgiveness, which hopefully leads to satisfaction, wisdom, and integrity. However, it's also possible that this reflection time may result in a dominating sense of bitterness as we regret our disappointments or lack of accomplishments.[5]

As psychology expanded in the 20th century, especially in America, subsequent generations of thinkers built on the work of their predecessors. One part of that evolving tree includes Dr. Lawrence Kohlberg and Dr. Carol Gilligan. Kohlberg built on the idea of stages of human development as they related to moral development. He postulated a

---

[5] Lachman, M. E., "Development in Midlife," *Annual Review of Psychology* 55 (2004): 305 331.

series of stages for how human beings grow in moral deliberation from an early stage oriented around avoiding punishment, through adapting to social norms, to a universal ethical principal. His graduate student, Dr. Carol Gilligan, in a groundbreaking book In a Different Voice, challenged Kohlberg's approach as lacking an understanding of the unique way in which women develop. Gilligan emphasized that men and women approach moral deliberation with varying assumptions. Her contribution to the field was groundbreaking at the time. She articulated an ethic of care and relational emphasis which she believed to be more dominant in women, hence the title of her work. "The different voice I describe is characterized not by gender but theme. Its association with women is an empirical observation and is primarily through women's voices that I trace its development. But this association is not absolute and the contrasts between male and female voices are presented here to highlight a distinction between two modes of thought and to focus on a problem of interpretation rather than to represent a generalization about either sex."[6] Gilligan's work has undergone criticism from recent thinkers, just as Erikson's and Jung's work have been critically evaluated. But what Gilligan brought forward challenged the assumption that men and women have the same approach to moral deliberation.

This is important for our study here because of the temptation to assume that men and women enter the second half of life as mere carbon copies of one another. Dr. Laurel Lippert Fox has identified some foundational differences for women approaching the second half of life. She highlights menopause, a post-parenting period of evolving roles. "As newer ways of understanding ourselves continue to emerge, one thing remains clear: If one's goal is to accurately represent the richness and diversity of women's developmental paths, postmodern perspectives offer a framework for understanding the complexity of the processes

---

[6] Gilligan, Carol. In a Different Voice: Psychological Theory and Women's Development,

involved."[7] We've moved from the idea of which theory is right or best for everyone to which one is right or best for the individual.

Celia Dodd, author of *The Empty Nest: Your Changing Family, Your New Direction*, describes her experience as a mother as the last of her three children moved out. She was pleased to see their successful launch, but grieved not only their absence, but the loss of her role as mother. "For me the empty nest transition was the most difficult, that's why I wrote a book about it. I really wish I'd known then what I know now, which is that the departure of your children leaves a gaping hole in your life, but that gradually develops into a creative space that you can fill with whatever you want."[8] Although pursuing a career, Dodd's experience of a midlife transition is centered more around her role in the family. "It started with the empty nest, trying to find my own way through that, and that certainly gave me reason for optimism."[9]

As we can see, there are numerous approaches to the models of human development, and each conceptually overlaps, as well as differentiates from one another. Erikson emphasizes the factors that impact human beings in the first part of life, while Jung is more concerned with the second half of life. Gilligan reminds us of the unique voice of women. Dodd and Lippert Fox add a social dimension to life's development. As the study of midlife or second half of life has grown in recent years, a legitimate question to ask might be: Is this true for anyone else on the planet, or is this just a white middle-class phenomenon? In 2008, researchers explored that very question in a study of people in over eighty countries. What did they find? Yes, indeed it is a global phenomenon from Albania to Zimbabwe. People often experience a transition point

---

[7] Laurel Lippert. "Women at Midlife: Implications for Theories of Women's Adult Development," *Journal of Counseling & Development*, (1997):16-22.

[8] https://www.retirementwisdom.com/podcasts/all-grown-up-celia-dodd/

[9] Ibid.

in their mid-40s.[10] University of Warwick economics professor Andrew Oswald, who led the study, is worth quoting at length here.

> Some people suffer more than others but in our data the average effect is large. It happens to men and women, to single and married people, to rich and poor, and to those with and without children. Nobody knows why we see this consistency.
>
> What causes this apparently U-shaped curve, and its similar shape in different parts of the developed and even often developing world, is unknown. However, one possibility is that individuals learn to adapt to their strengths and weaknesses, and in midlife quell their infeasible aspirations. Another possibility is that cheerful people live systematically longer. A third possibility is that a kind of comparison process is at work in which people have seen similar-aged peers die and value more their own remaining years. Perhaps people somehow learn to count their blessings.
>
> It looks from the data like something happens deep inside humans. Only in their 50s do most people emerge from the low period. But encouragingly, by the time you are 70, if you are still physically fit, then on average you are as happy and mentally healthy as a 20-year- old. Perhaps realizing that such feelings are completely normal in midlife might even help individuals survive this phase better.[11]

"It looks from the data like something deep happens inside humans." Thank you Professor, you have validated in the most 21st century of ways what religion, literature, philosophers, and psychologists have articulated for hundreds if not thousands of years. There is something deep inside us that happens. Call it a midlife crisis or the bottom of a U-shaped pattern or the beginning of the age of wisdom … but something does indeed happen.

---

[10] https://warwick.ac.uk/newsandevents/pressreleases/researchers_find_that/
[11] https://archive.nytimes.com/well.blogs.nytimes.com/2008/01/30/the-midlife-crisis-goes-global/

Changes – The theme of the second half of life

Change is indeed a constant throughout all of life. What's unique in the second half of life is that the changes seem to creep up on us. As a result, those established patterns of the first half of life get disrupted.

Physical Development – Any dinner table conversation among post-50-year-olds will undoubtedly include references to their physical well-being. These often appear in the form of jokes or lighted-hearted analogies but may also contain references to their hard-fought battles with cancer, heart disease, and other ailments. The reality of health issues such as cholesterol, chronic conditions, or disabilities dominate this age group, and differ according to gender. Women experience changes related to their reproductive capacity, including the cessation of menstruation and the accompanying hormonal changes. Men, too, experience changes in their physical ability in midlife as their stamina, agility, and virility decline. The former quarterback of the New England Patriots, Tom Brady, seems an outlier in this respect.

Our bodies are changing, and we accommodate a diminished sense of physical energy. There is plenty of evidence that continued physical exercise not only limits this decline in physical capacity; it may also rejuvenate well-being.[12]

Cognitive – Many adults experience life in the middle years with high mental capacity. This may diminish as one moves into later adulthood with name recall and other memory issues, but often these shortcomings are offset with a greater capacity for wisdom. A 58-year-old senior vice president of a large corporation recently reiterated a story about a young salesperson who was upset with a customer who was forcefully pursuing a partial rebate. My friend, the VP, explained to the young salesperson that while he was technically correct and the customer was annoyingly challenging, the total revenue of the contract far exceeded their complaint. "You are right, Sam. They should not

---

[12] Crowley & Lodge, Younger Next Year.

get the rebate they are seeking. But this client represents hundreds of thousands of dollars in annual revenue. We are not going to lose this contract over a $5,000 rebate. Call them up and authorize the rebate." This little vignette highlights one aspect of the wisdom and experience the older VP had acquired through the years. Our story also illustrates the other side of the coin regarding decreased cognitive capacity as we age. You'll note the VP addressed the salesman as Sam. The salesman's name was Sean.

Social – Much of middle adulthood centers around individuals' social and relational functioning. This includes families, work partners, friends we value as witnesses, and partners in our life endeavors. The nurturing of these relationships with shared interests are all central tasks of this period of life. If we have had a healthy ego development, personal identity, and resolution of previous-stage crises, we are better positioned to engage socially at this point in life.

As we enter the second half of life, it's not unusual for us to pare down the number of relationships we have. The first half of life's motto, "more is better," seems to be adjusted as we move into our 50s and 60s. Rather than acquiring many friends, we invest in a few to strengthen and deepen those relationships. Granted, there are exceptions to this pattern, particularly for more extroverted types of people, who seem to have an almost insatiable appetite for social connection. But, even among this crowd, there is a desire to deepen existing relationships rather than initiate new ones.

Emotional – We strengthen our emotional capacity during this period. Middle adulthood is a time of increased well-being, although the sources of happiness may vary by social class and race. However, midlife adults experience stress concerning multiple career demands, family demands, and internal questions around generativity versus stagnation. Whether we are parents attending to the needs of young children or adult children caring for older parents, our emotional and relational capacity is exercised regularly. If we have a strong sense of satisfaction with our life accomplishments, we tend to be more favorably disposed to move through this period of life with vitality. However, if our failures or losses dominate this period, we struggle with a sense of stagnation. I have often heard both men and women reference a feeling of being "stuck" in these middle years.

Since men have struggled to access and experience the range and nuance of their emotions throughout most of their lives, midlife can be an opportunity. Our culture seems slightly more willing to accept emotional expression by men as they age. The once stoic football coach now seems more capable of accessing his feelings for players. The hard-living plumber who recently became a grandfather feels his eyes moisten as he holds his granddaughter. There is an opportunity for men to gain some wisdom as they engage with long-dormant emotions.

Middle Adulthood and Spiritual Growth

In many ways, the Italian poet Dante was the first to articulate the peculiarities of the midlife passage:

> *Midway along the journey of our life*
> *I woke to find myself in a dark wood,*
> *for I had wandered off from the straight path.*[13]

Carl Jung is likely the first among modern psychologists to identify the midlife transition. He discovered it personally in his 30s and then noticed how many of his patients suffered from a spiritual problem during the middle of life. Jung observed the struggles of his patients along with his own turmoil. Maybe that is what led him to place such an emphasis on the second half of life. His concept of Individuation serves as the primary undertaking for this effort. This is a process of individual psychological and spiritual development. The "chief *dynamis*

---

[13] Dante Alighieri, *The Divine Comedy*

[power or energy or passion] from midlife on is the drive to grow the unique personality that the Self is impelling. This means that in the second half of life, the concerns of the ego become less important."[14]

The second half of life is focused on questions of ultimate value and meaning. If we focus on building an identity in the first half of life, establishing a career, finding a life partner in an intimate relationship, we shift in the second half of life to ask: What does all of this mean? People in the second half of life want to make sense of the entirety of their lives as they approach the end of life.

Jung uses the analogy of life as a single day. He describes the first half of life as the morning, the second half as the afternoon.

> Wholly unprepared, we embark upon the second half of life. Or are there perhaps colleges for forty-year-olds which prepare them for their coming life and its demands as the ordinary colleges introduce our young people to a knowledge of the world? No, thoroughly unprepared, we take the step into the afternoon of life; worse still, we take this step with the false assumption that our truths and ideals will serve us as hitherto. But we cannot live the afternoon of life according to the program of life's morning; for what was great in the morning will be little at evening, and what in the morning was true will at evening have become a lie.[15]

This quote illustrates Jung's attitude toward the second half of life as compared to the first half. Reading these quotes alone, one could interpret Jung as expressing almost a disdain for childhood, youth, and young adult development. However, I don't believe that is his intent. Instead, it was simply his view that the second half of life is where one discovers meaning and wisdom.

---

[14] Beebe, J.& Cambray J., & Kirsch, T., "What Freudians can Learn from Jung " *Psychoanalytic Psychology*. 18. (2001) 236.

[15] Jung, *The Portable Jung*, 16-17.

Erik Erikson's theory of a fully developed life stage model enhances Jung's ideas. In his model of human development, Erikson is clear that there are a series of tasks that must be achieved along the way to prepare people for a complete pattern of growth. For example, suppose we have not attained a healthy or mature level of personal identity. In that case, it's difficult to imagine how one could enter the second half of life asking questions of ultimate value and meaning. On the other hand, as Yale researcher Daniel Levinson has noted, some persons have significantly suffered in the first half of life and "lack the inner and outer resources for creating a minimally adequate life structure in middle adulthood. As a result, they face a middle age of constriction and decline."[16]

Since the second half of life orients us to questions of life's meaning, this inevitably leads us to engage with our world's great wisdom and spiritual traditions. By this, I am not suggesting going back to church or mosque or temple as a prescription for a midlife crisis, though that may be someone's choice. In the modern era, we have moved away from the notion that sacred institutions or ancient forms of mythology are the only unquestioned sources of wisdom and divine experience. Instead, what has occurred in our time is a shift toward the individual to discover what stirs their soul. Our task centers on exploring the sacred on our own, albeit with the help of guides and resources from various sources, including religion, philosophy, psychology, the arts, and literature.

Religious education professor James Fowler provides a useful framework for understanding the spiritual or faith development aspects of this stage of life. His seminal work *Stages of Faith* describes six stages of faith that human beings journey through over the course of a lifetime. The movement from the fantasy-filled world of the young child through a concrete interpretation of beliefs at adolescence and

---

[16] Levinson, D. J. et al, *The Seasons of a Man's Life*, 243.

the individualistic world view of young adults, Fowler says, leads us into midlife and beyond.

His fifth stage, our midlife stage which Fowler references with the awkward title "Conjunctive Faith," marks an ability to embrace nuance with the value of direct experience. We grow in our appreciation for symbols, myths, and meaningful experiences. We seek to reconcile the world as we know it, with all its faults, with an inner vision of transformation. We are changing and growing not only physically, cognitively, and emotionally, but also spiritually. There is a marked difference between earlier stages that included more either/or dichotomized logic in one's approach to faith matters. We move toward the more both/and approach that marks the entrance to midlife and old age. This ability to embrace nuance and dialogue within oneself and others is a rich achievement and a resource for the second half of life. Fowler prefers the term dialogical knowing. "In dialogical knowing, the multiplex structure of the world is invited to disclose itself."[17] In other words, one develops what the poet David Whyte calls "a conversational relationship with the world."[18]

Professor Nicola Slee offers an alternative view of women's faith development, suggesting that James Fowler's theory does not adequately account for women's experiences in their spiritual development. She means that women's faith development experiences may be better understood through alternative frameworks incorporating relational, embodied, and contextual aspects of spirituality. Slee also contends that Fowler's theory assumes a linear, sequential progression of faith development, which does not adequately capture the complexity and diversity of women's spiritual journeys. "Women's experiences of faith development are often more relational and embodied than men's, emphasizing the importance of community, empathy, and care."[19] In much

---

[17] Fowler, J. W., *Stages of Faith*, 185.

[18] Whyte, D. *Essentials*.

[19] Slee, *Women's Faith Development: Patterns and Processes*, 85.

of her work, Slee calls for a more inclusive and diverse approach to understanding faith development, one that considers the unique experiences of women and other marginalized groups.

Her emphasis on the unique experiences of women in their spiritual journeys is particularly poignant in the middle years. According to Slee, a dynamic and relational process characterizes their social and cultural contexts. She argues that women's spiritual growth is not linear but cyclical and recursive, as they encounter new challenges and opportunities for learning and transformation throughout their lives. Slee suggests that women's faith development is often disrupted in midlife by significant changes and transitions, such as menopause, empty nesting, or caregiving for aging parents. "Midlife is often a time of transition and change, when women may experience a sense of spiritual disorientation and a need to re-evaluate their lives and priorities."[20]

These challenges can lead to disorientation and reorientation, where women must re-evaluate their sense of identity, purpose, and values and may experience a sense of spiritual crisis or questioning. In response to these challenges, Slee proposes that women in midlife may engage in the process of "spiritual awakening," which involves a deeper and more embodied experience of spirituality. She suggests that this awakening emphasizes a movement towards greater authenticity, relationality, and connectedness and may include a shift in focus from external achievements and accomplishments to internal growth and well-being.

Professor Slee's theory of women's faith development emphasizes the importance of context and relationality in understanding women's spiritual journeys. She suggests that women's experiences of midlife can be a catalyst for transformation and growth and may lead to a more profound and integrated sense of spirituality. "The process of spiritual awakening involves a shift from external achievement to internal

---

[20] Slee, *The Faith Lives of Women and Girls: Qualitative Research Perspectives*, 11.

growth, from being oriented towards the needs of others to becoming more fully oneself."[21]

In midlife, the transition into this more conversational and nuanced way of approaching faith and spirituality can initially be unsettling for people. Both Levinson and Fowler reported examples of people, typically men, who struggled in this shift of thinking. However, the resources of a "conjunctive faith" engage the power of symbols alongside their conceptual meanings. "This includes the ability to engage paradox and the apparent contradictions. This stage strives to unify opposites in mind and experience."[22] As Slee has pointed out, this conversational and nuanced way of engaging life seems more natural to their lived experience. Paradox, living with apparent contradictions, and a movement toward internal growth echo much of the depth psychological tradition begun by Carl Jung.

Perhaps more than in any other school of thought, Jungian psychology employs metaphors, mythology, symbols, dreams, and various nuanced approaches. The study of archetypes (images and ideas of historical and cultural value) forms the basis for examining religious experience. It provides a context for a deeper look at spiritual development throughout the life cycle. At every stage of ego development, archetypes manifest themselves in ways appropriate to that stage of life.

Jung believed that attention to ultimate meaning was essential if people were to navigate the second half of life. "I am convinced that is hygenic ... to discover in death a goal toward which one can strive, and that shrinking away from it is something unhealthy and abnormal which robs the second half of life of its purpose."[23]

---

[21] Ibid, 16.

[22] Fowler, 198.

[23] Jung & Campbell, The Portable Jung, 21.

Numerous contemporary authors have proposed all manner of therapeutic, educational, and societal options for addressing the midlife transition. These include advice to join a local gym, start a hobby, provide better vacation packages for employees. Such activities may indeed offer symptom relief and even improve one's mental or physical well-being. I have become more attentive to these matters as I age. Regular, if not daily, exercise is an absolute in my life. This includes walking, bicycling, swimming, yard work. When combined with a healthy balanced diet and at least a few hearty laughs, I'm ready to go. Yet, the more profound questions around ultimate value, purpose, and meaning remain. As pointed out earlier, we now live in a time where the individual, not the sacred or secular institutions, is responsible for their inner landscape. This seems more compelling in the second half of life than at any other time. The resources we will explore in the coming chapters provide opportunities for making the journey in the afternoon of life a rich one.

Chapter 2

In Search of Wisdom

*It is quite true what philosophy says,
that life must be understood backwards.
But one forgets the other principle,
that it must be lived forward.*[1]

-Soren Kierkegaard, Danish Philosopher

We live in a culture that excels at the priorities of the first half of life. This emphasis has brought about incredible inventions, solutions, and achievements. In my former congregation, I knew a woman who died a day short of her 100th birthday. She had witnessed the full range of dramatic achievements during her lifetime. Her life spanned a series of dramatic changes that included the invention of airplanes, the development of antibiotics, and such innovations as the handheld computer. Those advances can be attributed to our society prioritizing an external material world view, competitive capitalism, and an expansive mindset.

We continue to encourage each generation to perpetuate this approach by emphasizing independence, getting a practical education, and launching a career that will bring financial rewards. Increasingly the subject areas of the arts and humanities suffer cuts from school budgets while investment in STEM (Science, Technology, Engineering and Mathematics) increases. The truth is we need the latter, but not at the expense of the former.

---

[1] Kierkegaard, *Journals and Notebooks, Volume 2*, 179.

My son told me of an exchange with an adult while in his final year of college.

"What's your major?" the adult asked.

"I'm a philosophy major," my son replied.

"Philosophy?" the man said, "What can you do with that?"

My son paused, looked at the gentleman, and with a disarming smile responded, "Oh, I don't know. Enjoy life."

This exchange illustrates our culture's emphasis on education. The purpose of four years of college, or service in the military, or any young adult activity, is focused on the useful, practical, and economically viable. But my son's quick wit provided a countercultural response that often occurs to us as we move through life. In case you are wondering, my son went on to become an attorney.

Although we can begin earlier in life, it's often in the second half that we pursue a life of meaning. Indeed, the pursuit of wisdom becomes a yearning. But what is wisdom?

Being the meaning-seeking, story-driven creatures we are, let's begin with a story to illustrate wisdom. Here is an old folktale that originates in Japan titled "The Mountain Where Old People Were Abandoned."

> Long ago, when people had reached the age of sixty and were unable to do anything, they were thrown into a mountain canyon. This was known as "sixty canyon abandonment."
>
> In a particular village, a farmer became sixty years old. Since the lord of the country had commanded it, the time had arrived for him to be thrown into the mountain canyon. The man's son *and daughter* took him and set off for the mountains. They continued farther and farther into the mountains. As they went along, the old man, being carried, broke off the tips of tree branches in order to mark the trail. "Father, Father, what are you doing that for? Is it so you can find your way back home?" the son and daughter asked.
>
> "No, it would be too bad if you were unable to find your way home," replied the father, "so I am marking the trail for you."

When they heard this, the son *and daughter* realized how kindhearted their father was, so they returned home with him. They hid the old man under the porch so that the lord would know nothing about it.

Now the lord of the country sometimes commanded his subjects to do very difficult things. One day he gathered all the farmers of the village together and said, "You must bring me a rope woven from ashes."

All the farmers were very troubled, knowing that they could not possibly weave a rope from ashes. The young farmers whom we just mentioned went back home, called to their father under the porch, and said, "Today, the lord commanded everyone to bring a rope woven from ashes. How can we do this?"

"You must weave a rope very tightly, then carefully burn it until it turns to ashes: then you can take it to the lord," said the old man.

The young farmers, happy to get this advice, did just as they were told, made a rope of ashes, and took it to the lord. None of the other farmers could do it, and so these young farmers alone had carried out the lord's instructions. For this, the lord praised them highly.

Next, the lord commanded, "Everyone must bring a conch shell with a thread passed through it."

The young farmers went to their father again and asked him what they should do. "Take a conch shell and point the tip toward the light; then take a thread and stick a piece of rice on it. Next, give the rice to an ant and make it crawl into the mouth of the shell; in this way, you can get the thread through."

The young farmers did as they were told and got the thread through the conch shell. Then, they took the shell to the lord, who was much impressed. "How were you able to do such a difficult thing?" he asked.

The young farmers replied: "Actually, we were supposed to throw our old father down into the mountain canyon, but we felt so sorry for him that we brought him back home and hid him under the porch. The things that you asked us to do were so difficult that we had to ask our father how to do them. So, we have done them as he told us and brought them to you."

When the lord heard this, he was very impressed and realized that old people are very wise and should be well taken care of. After that, he commanded that the "sixty canyon abandonment" be stopped.[2]

This is an old story from Japan, but versions appear in India and other parts of Asia dating back to the 11th century. A version in European folklore is sometimes ascribed to King Solomon. It's a powerful story that captures the human imagination, and like many oral traditions, it has been told and retold. I'm retelling it here because I believe it is a story for our time.

Many of those who have much life experience possess wisdom. While that wisdom may be perceived as odd or even weird, it is needed. In our time, we have come to worship the young. Don't get me wrong; the young have much to offer, including energy, a commitment to the external world, and a willingness to innovate. The challenge for our time is that while focusing on the young, we have abandoned the old.

"It is quite true what philosophy says, that life must be understood backwards. But one forgets the other principle, that it must be lived forward." As a tale for our time, it convicts our culture's attitude toward elders. We view them as expendable, out of touch and lacking value. If you doubt me, just browse the greeting card section at your local pharmacy. Here is an industry rife with denigrating messages about aging in America. But the children in the story display what Carol Gilligan called an "ethic of care."[3] While at first they are motivated by compassion for their father, they later realize this old man has wisdom to teach them. I find it curious that the story has the old man hidden

---

[2] Dorson, *Folktales Told around the World*, 243.

[3] Gilligan, *In a Different Voice: Psychological Theory and Women's Development*.

under the porch. These ancient stories tell us more about ourselves than we realize. The underworld, the lower level, the underside of the porch often represent the place of soul activity, what Jung called the unconscious. As each progression of tasks and challenges is demanded by the warlord of their village, the resolutions are delivered by the man of wisdom who lives underneath the house.

Part of finding wisdom in the second half of life is searching the lower regions of our own inner house. Wisdom is not always found exclusively in our mind where we think through problems. Sometimes we are summoned to another level. Some modern-day phrases that hint at this source of wisdom include, "I had a gut feeling" or "Deep inside I knew the right answer."

Another view of wisdom worth mining is found in the Hebrew scriptures. Those books of the Bible with titles like Job, the Psalms, Proverbs, and the Songs of Solomon (not to mention fragments scattered throughout other portions of the Hebrew Bible) contain a wealth of learning.

"The fear of the Lord is the beginning of wisdom." (Proverbs 9:10) Even people less familiar with the Jewish or Christian religions have likely heard this phrase. Yet, we are not served well by the translations we've inherited through the years. "Fear of God" suggests a deity to be scared of, and we should live in dread of any engagement. When I'm afraid of something or someone, I attempt to avoid and run the other way. How is wisdom connected with fear?

The Hebrew word *yirah* appears often in the Old Testament and has a range of meanings. Sometimes it refers to the fear we feel in anticipation of danger or pain, but it can also mean "awe" or "reverence," and can connote wonder, amazement, mystery, gratitude, and admiration. Thus the "fear of the Lord" includes an overwhelming sense of glory, worth, and beauty. This suggests that the beginning of wisdom can be found by leaning into an awe-filled, mysterious, and beautiful Spirit.

Dr. Wil Gafney of Brite Divinity School reminds us of the feminine nature of wisdom in this section of Proverbs, and elsewhere in the scriptures. Traditionally, Wisdom is considered to be female, largely because the noun for wisdom, *chokmah* in Hebrew, is grammatically feminine; this is also true of the ancient Greek *sophia*. That's significant for our understanding of this whole section of Proverbs because Wisdom is the hostess of a giant banquet, and all are welcome. Everyone is invited into this Wisdom feast. Wisdom in the mystical literature of Judaism called the Kabbalah conveys an assortment of characteristics including beauty, eternity, splendor, kindness, understanding, sovereignty, power, and divine presence. Wisdom extends her hospitality and hopes that all who come to the feast will practice wisdom in a variety of ways. The women (Exodus 35:26) and men (Exodus 31:6) who craft the Tabernacle in the wilderness are all called wise; in Deuteronomy 4:6, if Israel keeps the Torah they will be a "wise and discerning people;" in 2 Samuel 20:22, the wise woman who led her city seems to be the governing official who saves her people from certain death by shrewd and lethal political dealing; and of course the wisdom of Solomon was legendary, 1 Kings 4:29.[4]

My view is that we need to bring a balance to our worldview, and the wisdom of the elder who has crossed the threshold of midlife, who has learned *yirah*, is a contribution we cannot avoid or dismiss. Of course, not everyone is ready or willing to cross the threshold. Some prefer, despite their aging bodies, to cling to youth. We see those people dressing, acting, grooming as if they were 19 years of age, despite walking in 58-year-old bodies. But for those who choose to embrace the second half of life as an opportunity to cultivate some weird wisdom, I believe it is possible to gain fulfillment and a mature spirituality, and to contribute to a better world.

---

[4] Gafney, https://www.workingpreacher.org/commentaries/revised-common-lectionary/ordinary-20-2/commentary-on-proverbs-91-6

Here's the answer: There is no answer. Life is not a question to be answered. If that were the case, well, it would be over. Life is a question to be lived, as Kierkegaard said, not backwards, but forwards. This is at the heart of the wisdom we seek.

In 1993, I arrived at a small congregation in Charlestown, Rhode Island. I began a men's breakfast that met on Saturday mornings at a local greasy spoon. Each week several guys ranging in age from 35 to 75 would imbibe a diet of heavy cholesterols, heated caffeine, and conversation about a range of topics from sports to landscaping to philosophy and religion. I left the group with both a stomachache and a headache most of the time, but the camaraderie was worth it. One Saturday, a 50-year-old guy hung around afterward, clearly wanting to engage me privately. We stood outside, leaning against his pickup truck. He proceeded to pour out his life to me. All the disappointments, all the infidelities, all the mismanagement of money, all the shattered dreams just rolled out before us. It just rolled one right after the other. I listened. He described himself as a mess and needed to talk to someone. I agreed to find him a professional to help explore significant factors in his life.

Just before we parted ways, he turned and said to me: "Pastor, just one question."

"Sure," I responded. "I figure since you're a minister, you probably know the answer to this, but what's it all about?" I must have looked puzzled because he followed up by saying, "You know, this life. What's the point?"

I was 34 years old. He had a couple of decades on me. A thousand thoughts went through my mind, but not a single one made it out of my mouth. I must have looked stunned. Finally, after a long silence, he said: "Yeah, I know. I don't know either. But if you ever find the answer, let me know."

I lost touch with that man through the years. Nearly thirty years later, I've finally landed on a response, which is this book. But if I could formulate a response and go back in time to that gravel parking lot outside the Hungry Haven on that cool, sunny autumn morning, I'd say, "I don't think there is a single answer to that question. But I think that is the point. The answer is in the living of life with all its disappointments and achievements, complexities, and wonders. We live the questions along with the answers. And at the end, we look back and say, 'Oh, now I get it, it was about living a generous and intentional life.' That's wisdom, as weird as that may sound."

On the Turning of my 63rd Year

Hiking the Carter Preserve
On the trail
Marked by granite and moss,
Glacial rubble from the Pleistocene.
To the west
the sun moves from zenith to landfall.
A breeze tickles the white pines and the birch.
Above me, the cumulus gather.
For a coming storm
Or the passing of one.

Section Two

Chapter 3

Wonder

"Wisdom begins in Wonder."

- Plato

The ancient Greek philosopher Plato actually said, "Wonder is the feeling of a philosopher, and philosophy begins in wonder."[1] In particular, wonder is an attitude, a posture, and a perspective on life. There is Wonder, the noun, as in "The pyramids of Egypt are a wonder to behold." But that's for our next chapter. Here I'm thinking of Wonder as a verb.

I wonder why that teenager across the street is sitting on the curb looking so sad?

I wonder how the universe came into being?

I wonder what's for dinner?

From the seemingly day-to-day to the big questions of life, Wonder moves us from passivity to an active engagement with it all.

Wonder is a predisposition toward surprise, curiosity, and the expectation that you might learn something. It celebrates doubt and inquisitiveness, but mostly it leans into a posture that there is something more. This yearning for something more is central to wisdom, as Plato

---

[1] Plato, *Dialogs of Plato*, http://data.perseus.org/citations/urn:cts:greekLit:tlg0059.tlg006.perseus-eng1:155d

reminds us. When we mindfully reflect upon our lives and relationships, practicing self-inquiry and curiosity, we are invited to embark upon the path of wisdom.

In fact, of all the characteristics of weird wisdom that we are exploring in this book, wonder just might be the single most important one. Why? Because Wonder leads us into a life where discovery, adventure and fresh perspectives abound. Those are the same qualities we experienced in our childhood. At that time, every day was filled with a sense of possibility. That same sense will serve us well in the second half of life.

Human beings have unique capabilities among all the creatures on this planet. We can reflect, imagine, explore. This is all a form of Wonder. How did the great religions come into being? How did the inventions of the past one hundred years appear? How is it possible that, unlike any other species, we have been able to lengthen our life spans, grow in stature and strength, and change our environment? The potential to impact all of life emerges out of Wonder.

And yet, how many people have we encountered who seem to have surrendered their capacity for Wonder? It's as if they turned their imaginative powers off decades earlier, and all that remains is a life of golf, TV, and Florida. Without a robust engagement of the act of Wonder, modern people live their lives as if the only reality is that which they can see, hear, or touch. This materialistic outlook, while certainly a significant part of life, has its limits.

"In modern Western society, we have reached a point at which we try to get by without acknowledging inner life. We act as though there were no unconscious, as though we could live full lives by completely fixating on the external, material world."[2]

---

[2] Johnson, *Inner Work: Using Your Dreams and Active Imagination for Personal Growth*, 1.

Many of us in North America have become devoted to the philosophy of materialism, which teaches that nothing exists except matter and its movements. There's a robust debate in philosophical circles about the limits of the philosophy of materialism, and I'm particularly fond of the British philosopher Mary Midgely, whose work challenges this school of thought. How can a reader not love a writer whose self-critical analysis argues that philosophy is like plumbing, something that nobody notices until it goes wrong? "Then suddenly, we become aware of some bad smells, and we have to take up the floorboards and look at the concepts of even the most ordinary piece of thinking. The great philosophers ... noticed how badly things were going wrong, and made suggestions about how they could be dealt with."[3]

But the materialistic worldview is the one you and I hold. For a long time, this worldview shaped us to believe that only the visible world is the totality of existence. Yes, it's been with us since the dawn of human civilization, but today the materialistic world view dominates our conscious thought. The ancient hunter on the plains of North America viewed the charging buffalo as a concrete reality to be dealt with, hence the origins of a fight, flight, or freeze response to real dangers. However, that same hunter also held a worldview that somehow the buffalo possessed a spiritual nature or perhaps was brought to that moment by a divine essence. Today, the average person in society views the buffalo as a source of protein in a bison burger. There is a utilitarian quality to the buffalo. In other words it's simply meat to fuel the activities of the day. Not to mention the naïve tourist visiting Yellowstone National Park has little or no concept of the power of such an animal, hence the annual reports of impaled tourists thinking they are at a theme park.

Even those enthusiastic followers of that first-century Jewish rabbi found themselves in this quandary in Jerusalem. Following his torture

---

3 Else, Liz "Mary, Mary, quite contrary," *New Scientist*, 3 November 2001.

and death via a hideous form of capital punishment, Jesus appears to appear in the days following his death. But, one of the followers didn't check his text messages that day and missed the viewing. After he hears the passionate declarations of his colleagues, he utters the most modern of exclamations: unless I see the evidence, I'm not convinced of this charade. The biblical narrative is more dramatic and poetic: "Unless I see the nail holes in his hands, put my finger in the nail holes, and stick my hand in his side, I won't believe it." (John 20:25 The Message)

After centuries of scholarship, what we know about drafting these accounts is significant. The Gospels are not eyewitness accounts; they're retellings of stories likely handed down through several decades of oral tales and notes on crumpled Starbucks napkins. So, what we have tells us a great deal about the communities where these collections were codified into a written text. This story of Thomas (so-called doubting Thomas) is one of the truly great gifts to the church and all of humanity. I reason that it raises a profound question that goes back at least 2,000 years. Doubt was a part of the early movement of religions emerging after that rabbi from Galilee.

Thomas was not the first modern human to express doubt. There is ample evidence of healthy doubt in the writings of the pre-Socratic philosophers through Aristotle and on to the Cynics of Roman antiquity.[4] But Thomas codified in the Christian mindset the idea that doubt was not a value to be dismissed. Undoubtedly, Thomas might be rethought of as "Curious Thomas." This early follower of the man from Nazareth embodies an archetype of doubt and wonder, thus giving followers of Jesus permission today to engage in curiosity and wonder.

Consider Thomas's reaction earlier in John's gospel when Jesus predicts his imminent departure. Thomas responds, "Lord, we do not know where you are going. How can we know the way?" (John 14:5)

---

[4] Ornella Sinigaglia, *Maize* May 31, 2021.

Does Thomas already know what Jesus means and is expressing doubt, or does he not get it yet and is simply wondering out loud?

Thomas is a curious disciple of Jesus, yes, pun intended. Outside of a few references and quotes in John's gospel, we know very little about him, other than that he was a twin. But there are many traditions and narratives about Thomas. According to modern Syrian Christians living in Kerala, India, Thomas visited that region in 52 CE. He established an early Christian community along the coast of Malabar. A millennium and a half later, in 1498, the Portuguese explorer Vasco da Gama landed his ships off the coast and discovered, much to his surprise, a thriving Christian community. While the influence of European colonialism disturbed the Thomasine churches, there are theological and liturgical remnants that reveal a vital and robust Eastern Indian Orthodox style of Christianity.[5]

According to tradition, Thomas made his way not only to India but also to Egypt and the surrounding Mediterranean communities during the first two centuries. His name is associated with a collection of Gnostic sayings compiled by scribes in the first century. The so-called Gnostic Gospel According to Thomas is a collection of aphorisms, teachings, and parables of Jesus the Christ.[6] The Coptic text scrolls discovered in the Egyptian desert in 1945 date back to the period of early Christianity.[7] The collection of sayings has a few parallels to commonly known parables of Jesus but mainly differs in approach, tone, and meaning. A

---

[5] Zacharia https://www.smithsonianmag.com/travel/how-christianity-came-to-india-kerala-180958117/

[6] Those first one hundred to two hundred years featured a plethora of religious and philosophical engagement. There was not one Christian faith. There were many ideologies. The Gospel of Thomas has received much attention, and scholars date it as early as 60 CE to as late as 140 CE. This places it in the same time frame as the four Gospels of Matthew, Mark, Luke, and John, all compiled into their final form between 70 CE and 110 CE.

[7] Valantasis, *The Gospel of Thomas*.

few examples of the more than 114 verses might help us ask questions and wonder about another side of the Jesus narrative.

> In verse 19 of the Gospel of Thomas Jesus said, "Blessed is he who came into being before he came into being. If you become my disciples and listen to my words, these stones will minister to you. For there are five trees for you in Paradise which remain undisturbed summer and winter and whose leaves do not fall. Whoever becomes acquainted with them will not experience death."
>
> (verse 24) His disciples said to him, "Show us the place where you are, since it is necessary for us to seek it." He said to them, "Whoever has ears, let him hear. There is light within a man of light, and he lights up the whole world. If he does not shine, he is darkness."
>
> (verse 36) Jesus said, "Do not be concerned from morning until evening and from evening until morning about what you will wear."
>
> (verse 48) Jesus said, "If two make peace with each other in this one house, they will say to the mountain, 'Move Away,' and it will move away."
>
> (verse 70) Jesus said, "That which you have will save you if you bring it forth from yourselves. That which you do not have within you will kill you if you do not have it within you."[8]

In these verses, you can see similarities to the sayings of Jesus in Matthew's Gospel, as an example. But you can also see the differences.

---

[8] Gospel of Thomas, Translated by Thomas O. Lambdin
https://www.marquette.edu/maqom/Gospel%20of%20Thomas%20Lambdin.pdf

It's improbable that this collection actually comes from Thomas, one of the original disciples. But it is curious that his name, of all the disciples' names, came to be associated with these sayings. Was it easier for an early scribe to attribute it to the doubting, curious, pondering, and wondering disciple? Is there something in the spirit of the Jesus tradition that suggests a value of curiosity, and Thomas personifies that archetype? Why is it that Thomas is a name associated with far-off travel to exotic places like India and alternative versions of Christianity like Gnosticism? Are we to learn something from Thomas? Is curiosity a value embraced by the early church? Should it be recovered for our time and our lives?

"If you bring forth what is within you, what you bring forth will save you. If you do not bring forth what is within you, what you do not bring forth will destroy you."[9] This translation by Elaine Pagels captures one possible answer. And it serves us well as we seek to find the Weird Wisdom needed for our lives today.

From Happiness to Wonder

Enshrined in the preamble to the American Declaration of Independence of 1776 might be the most unfortunate of all of Thomas Jefferson's writings: "We hold these truths to be self-evident, that all men are created equal, that they are endowed by their Creator with certain unalienable rights, that among these are Life, Liberty, and the pursuit of Happiness." It's that last word that I maintain is unfortunate. Why? Because almost 250 years later, views on happiness have changed. Today, many of us believe that the goal of life is to be happy in an emotional state of endorphin euphoria, constant and forever. Personally, I think that sounds exhausting. To make things worse, it's tied in with

---

[9] Elaine Pagels in From Jesus to Christ.
https://www.pbs.org/wgbh/pages/frontline/shows/religion/story/thomas.html

an understanding of liberty which the average person interprets as "I'm free to do whatever I want." The collision of those two belief systems leads to the pursuit of happiness as a drive for narcissistic self-aggrandizement.

But Jefferson had something else in mind. According to Kathleen Kennedy Townsend, "The story goes that Jefferson, on the advice of Benjamin Franklin, substituted the phrase "pursuit of happiness" for the word "property," which was favored by George Mason. Franklin thought that "property" was too narrow a notion."[10] Even Mason had a broader definition as he wrote in the Virginia Declaration of Rights in 1776: "the enjoyment of life and liberty, with the means of acquiring and possessing property, and pursuing and obtaining happiness and safety."[11] While the "pursuit of happiness" has a more attractive ring than "property," we remain in the realm of material well-being. Yet, as Daniel Kahneman and other researchers have shown, people earning more than $75,000 per year intuitively know that more income does not equal life satisfaction.[12] This seems especially true for those in the second half of life. So, the calling of Wonder ringing in our hearts and souls is for the pursuit of something that will reignite our very being.

What would have happened if Jefferson had ignored Franklin's advice and gone in a different direction? What if that famous sentence had read, " ... among these are life, liberty, and the pursuit of wonder." Granted, an improbable decision on Jefferson's part. But this is the book where such playfulness is allowed and encouraged.

A life lived in pursuit of Wonder might yield a form of happiness if we redefine our expectations around that problematic word.

---

[10] https://www.theatlantic.com/business/archive/2011/06/the-pursuit-of-happiness-what-the-founders-meant-and-didnt/240708/

[11] https://www.archives.gov/founding-docs/virginia-declaration-of-rights

[12] https://content.time.com/time/magazine/article/0,9171,2019628,00.html

The website *Pursuit of Wonder* describes it well.[13] "Wonder is a feeling of curiosity and appreciation inspired by something beautiful, unfamiliar, or inexplicable. We produce content in hopes of inciting that feeling." Through over one hundred short YouTube videos, *Pursuit of Wonder* delves into the questions people hunger to explore, from the profoundly confusing to the simply obvious. Some titles include:

How Deep Does the Ocean Really Go?
The Philosophy of Socrates (& Plato)
Why We're All Anxious & Weird
The Mystery of Déjà Vu
The Art of Loneliness

What strikes me about this collection of topics is the absolute openness to the pursuit of learning. The determining factor of a spiritually mature person is one's ability to hold the tension of ambivalence and paradox. When we face the strain of this uncertain life, we often attempt to relieve that anxiousness through control and security. Unfortunately, those efforts often create an illusion that we are the masters of this world. They also generate problematic tensions with those around us, not to mention with that deeper soul within us. The antidote to anxiety is not in efforts to control but in our openness to Wonder - to live with contradiction, ambivalence, and nuance.

I've often told stories of my struggles and frustrations with challenging people and situations. A friend once remarked, "Whenever these things happen to me, I try to ask myself what is it that God wants me to learn from this encounter?" Note this is not suggesting that God is the cause of his frustrations, nor is it a variation of the naive "everything happens for a reason." Both reduce the sacred to an anthropomorphic spirit open to manipulation by human beings. Instead, my friend seeks an inner exploration, an openness to what life

---

[13] https://pursuitofwonder.com/

is brining into our midst. This is an embrace of wonder. As the write Francis Weller says, "Welcoming everything that comes to us is the challenge. This is the secret to being fully alive."[14]

The more we intentionally focus on Wonder and its accompanying questions, the more we experience our lives as meaningful. Indeed, this is what makes the second half of life so rich. This is the time to engage the questions of life. In the first half of life, we sought the answers needed to establish our credentials and standing in the world. All of that was required to get us to this point, but now we ask different questions.

What questions might lead us further and deeper along the path of discovering what this grand experiment of our lives might mean? Among the questions that might draw us along:

- Is my life connected to something larger than my day-to-day living?
- If so, what is that something larger? If not, where might one begin to discover or rediscover a largeness within life?
- Have I remembered to love and serve those around me?
- What are my fears? And how might I face them, despite the risk? What will be the reward?
- It's been said that 90 percent of life is just showing up. Where do I need to show up?
- Since everyone knows how to suffer, how might that suffering be a doorway to meaning?

The exploration of these questions is an act of curiosity and Wonder.

Stephen Aizenstat, American psychotherapist, describes his approach to life and dreams, which we will explore in a future chapter.

---

[14] Weller, *The Wild Edge of Sorrow: Rituals of Renewal and the Sacred Work of Grief*, 9.

To live a life enriched by a curious mind animates both body and spirit. Since I was a little boy, I've been curious about my dreams. As I grew older, my curiosity extended to waking life, as if the world was a dream. What I have found over the decades is that both my professional and social life are enhanced when I host curiosity.

I was reflecting on this phenomenon today as I was making an otherwise routine trip to the store. Instead of taking the familiar route, you know, the most efficient way, the course that is now coded into my internal GPS, I did something very different. This morning, rather than going on automatic pilot, I drove on the back roads, through neighborhoods that were unfamiliar to me. Oh my. Everything slowed down, and I took lots of time to notice. A quiet joy filled my being. I remembered—the world waits to be met by our curiosity. The spirits of place, the souls of things, the life sparks of creatures, including people, awaken when met by our curiosity.[15]

When we see something that defies a pattern, it ignites curiosity. Most of us lead lives of routine. We have our patterns that repeat daily. This gives us a strong sense of security and comfort. Your pattern may involve a daily habit of waking up at 6:00 a.m., eating the same thing for breakfast every day, and regularly departing for work by 8:15 a.m. You drive the same route and stop at the same coffee shop. But then, one day, you notice something out of the ordinary. It might be a sign, a new building, or a homeless person standing at the light. This ignites a curiosity within you.

University of Illinois physicist Nadya Mason explores the interaction between human beings and technology. Her work is the kind of research that makes my brain hurt. She is super-intelligent. She is also super-curious. Her 2019 TED Talk "How to Spark your Curiosity,

---

[15] Aizenstat https://dreamtending.com/blog/volume-xxxviii/

Scientifically" explores how curiosity is a primary way that human beings come to understand how the world works and what our place is in it.[16] She describes how a simple encouragement of school children to dismantle an Etch-a-Sketch® stimulated an interest in experiments. Mason hopes that this engaged curiosity is life-enriching.

Curiosity is one of the most discussed topics in the study of human behavior. We have learned that it is innate from birth, as illustrated by the phrase, childlike curiosity. We know it is essential to survival in the natural world. That cute, curious bear cub quickly learns the impact of sticking a paw into that honey pot in the bees' nest. Many successful leaders attribute their success to sustaining their childlike curiosity. But many people's sense of curiosity tends to wane or deteriorate as they age. We all know people who seem to stop. They stop learning, stop trying new foods, and stop listening to new music. They seem to lose interest in growing. I'm here to remind you that curiosity is integral to all we do in life, at every stage, and perhaps even more so in the second half of life. From innovation to creativity, motivation, leadership, and a meaningful life, curiosity is a critical difference-maker. It distinguishes between living a full life and merely existing.

"I think, at a child's birth, if a mother could ask a fairy godmother to endow it with the most useful gift, that gift would be curiosity."
— Eleanor Roosevelt

Throughout this chapter, I've used the words Wonder and curiosity interchangeably. In many ways, they are pretty similar. But not for Canadian philosopher John Vervaeke. He suggests that there is a difference, and an important one. "Curiosity suggests I'm lacking something, and it's oriented toward a solution to a problem. But wonder

---

[16] https://youtu.be/OMDVTZ-ycaY

is to put oneself into the momentum of mystery. You are trying to enter into a right relationship into the depth of reality."[17]

Vervaeke suggests that marketing departments in the business community love curiosity. However, Wonder is something wholly other. Wonder walks in the realm of mystery, imagination, and those aspects of life that seem a bit beyond the threshold of what we can know, touch, and taste. Vervaeke points to the world of spirituality and its role in Wonder. "One of the proper jobs of both ancient philosophy and religion is to continually restore people to the capacity to wonder."[18]

In the next chapter, we explore another aspect of Wonder. We now move from Wonder the verb to Wonder the noun, which I call enchantment.

---

[17] Vervaeke & Jonathan Pageau, Curiosity and Wonder Interview https://youtu.be/mrdJJCKkwdI

[18] ibid

Chapter 4

Enchantment

I have always tried to live by the 'awe principle.' That is: Can I find awe, wonder and enchantment in the most mundane things conceivable?[1]

-Craig Hatkoff

    You remember when you were young, the world was filled with wonder, and yes, even magic. As a young boy playing baseball with friends in the neighborhood, this occurred to me. Most of the kids were older than I and therefore stronger and more talented in sports. Consequently, it should not surprise everyone that I was the regular right fielder batting ninth. One afternoon in the large vacant lot near our home in southern California, I assumed my regular spot in right field. Typically, this meant a great deal of time watching the game with no activity for me. However, this day was very different and affected me for years to come.

    A friend of one of the neighborhood regulars joined us for the pickup game, and to everyone's surprise, when he stood at the plate, we saw something different. He batted leftie. I'd never qualify to replace Vin Scully, the famous Los Angeles Dodgers broadcaster, but in my head, I heard Scully narrating our sandlot scrimmage. "Now, batting third is Juan Cavatelli. But wait, folks, we have a southpaw coming to the plate. This might finally give the right fielder Jimmy Hazelwood some action."

    On his first at-bat, Juan grounded a single to right field. Later he popped out to me for an easy catch, but on his third at-bat, the visiting

---

[1] Hatkoff, https://www.fastcompany.com/3031100/from-arrogance-and-failure-to-helping-create-the-tribeca-film-festival

leftie hit a screaming line drive that sailed way over my head. As I ran to retrieve the ball, I knew it would be a home run because young Juan had already demonstrated his speed on the bases. Instead, the ball hit the ground and rolled underneath the dense brush that served as the right-field bleachers. I crawled underneath in search of the baseball, scaring off a small horned toad lizard in the process. I finally reached the ball deep underneath the brush. It was dark and cool, and then something happened.

I can't explain it, but it was as if time stood still. Silence surrounded me. To this day, I can smell the earth, damp and cool. I was transported not to another location but to, dare I say it, another dimension or perhaps another frame of mind. It seemed as if the whole universe had paused. I was surrounded by silence, darkness, and a still small voice that whispered the word "stillness." At this moment, I felt calm and peaceful. My concentration was broken when suddenly I heard my friends yelling, breaking my attention. "Did you find the ball?" they hollered. I scrambled out and tossed it back so that play could resume.

I'm not sure what happened on that day, and all these years later, I'm still at a loss for words to describe my experience. But the impact of that moment remains with me and reemerges from time to time. It fostered an appreciation for the mysterious, wonderful, and inexplicable in me. I now understand it as my first mystical experience, a moment of enchantment.

I've chosen enchantment as an alternative word to describe this yearning people have in their lives for something larger than themselves. I needed a term that was unusual to force you out of your typical categories. OK, let's be honest. I also needed a word starting with the letter E to fit the acronym of WEIRD.

Over the years, I've listened to many people describe moments of enchantment. An older gentleman shared an experience of hearing a voice say, "Remember your family" when he was a young man focused on his career. That experience transformed how he lived and paid attention to his wife and two daughters. A young teenage woman revealed her experience of seeing an angel accompany her to school as a young child when she felt threatened by older kids. A young man told me of a series of dreams he had of his deceased grandfather in which his "papa" guided him on some important life choices.

Enchantment is an unusual word for what I'm describing, but I believe it captures a part of the weird wisdom necessary to navigate the second half of life.

German social scientist Max Weber accurately described the modern era: "The fate of our times is characterized by rationalization and intellectualization and, above all, the disenchantment of the world."[2] This quote from a lecture in 1917 outlines what we might call a loss of the spiritual dimension of life. We are adept at logic, productivity, and manipulating things, including the biosphere. The results are amazing. Since Weber's lecture, lifespan has doubled, antibiotics lengthen lives, our homes provide comfort and safety. Most people living in North America lead lives even the kings and queens of previous generations could only imagine. If Solomon were transported to my home in Rhode Island, he would assume my wife and I were royalty. All this material acquisition and achievement shifted our thinking, for many of us now believe that the rational, materialistic world is all that matters. Yet, despite our incredible external achievements, modern people seem uneasy, unhappy, perhaps even depressed. Sigmund Freud may have been right when he wrote *Civilization and its Discontents*. Having achieved the dream of material well-being in the late modern era, are all of us equating the rational, materialistic world with the Kingdom of God?

Perhaps that is why we are seeing interest in the paranormal, astrology, the mysticism of the Eastern and Western religions, tarot

---

[2] Weber, *From Max Weber Essays in Sociology*, 129-156.

reading, and even hallucinogenic pharmacology. It seems we are moving away from a strictly rational and materialistic understanding of life, and what is emerging is a new emphasis on the spiritual. As a result, we are experiencing "the undoing of disenchantment." In my view ours is a time of post-disenchantment. Having deconstructed the religions and mythologies that brought us into the modern world, we find ourselves yearning for the mystery, the wonder of life.

I'm not advocating returning to some pre-modern worldview where hunter-gatherers offered sacrifices to ensure a good crop or the arrival of rain. On the contrary, human beings have significantly benefited from the modern worldview. Modern medicine, democracy, and indoor plumbing come to mind, among many other advantages. But the modern era also desacralized our world. Thinkers like Marx and Freud believed that religion would fade from human existence. The superstitious thinking of so-called pre-modern people would no longer dominate the modern mind. Science would replace all of that, and humanity would move into a truly golden era. But during the last hundred years scientific advances have made possible horrific wars, mass murder, nuclear weapons, environmental degradation, and the real possibility that we human beings can destroy our planet and ourselves. We all now know that science, like religion, can also be used for good or for ill. But the heart and soul of modern humanity still need attention. Those societies that tried to squelch all expressions of religious life experienced a surprise. Spiritual exploration has proliferated underground in both China and the former Soviet Union. Here in the United States, while institutional forms of religious life have declined, other yearnings for a connection with the transcendent continue to expand.

Carl Jung wrote extensively about what he described as the religious impulse or instinct within each human being. Just as Freud talked about a sexual instinct and Alfred Adler articulated a power drive within each of us, Jung emphasized a spiritual force. He believed we possess an innate yearning to connect with the holy, the divine. "The understanding of religion [of the man of today] is made considerably more difficult owing to the lack of explanations ... If, despite this, he has still not discarded all his religious convictions, this is because the religious impulse rests on an instinctive basis and is therefore a specifically human function."[3]

There are numerous other places in Jung's writings, lectures, and interviews where he articulates various perspectives on this subject. In a BBC television interview, when asked if he believes in God, Jung claims that he knows God is real. He doesn't need to believe, because he has had a real encounter with God. Later a viewer of that BBC interview, asked Jung to define what he meant by God. Jung provides a rather unique definition. "To this day God is the name by which I designate all things which cross my willful path violently and recklessly, all things which upset my subjective views, plans and intentions and change the course of my life for better or worse."[4]

One of the critical aspects of the weird wisdom that will be of tremendous benefit for you as you navigate the second half of life is embracing the spiritual dimension of life, which I call enchantment. Let's be clear on what I'm not saying first. I'm not saying you need to get religion and make your way back to the church, synagogue, or temple. However, you may choose that route if you wish. I'm also not saying you need to believe in a deity that dresses in flowing robes, keeps an account of everyone's behavior while seated on a throne surrounded by flying winged creatures singing adorations as if the Creator is so insecure "he" needs all that attention.

I am suggesting that cultivating an openness to a non-material dimension to everyday life will be of service to you in this chapter of your life. Jung called it the Transcendent function. Others have given it various names such as the spiritual dimension, an attitude of wonder, the

---

[3] Jung "Psychology & Religion" vol. 11, para 544

[4] Jung, *Selected Letters of C.G. Jung, 1909-1961*, 183.

universe, and others simply God. That last phrase seems to limit some people's view of what I'm suggesting, which is ironic. Perhaps this aspect of life, which I'm calling enchantment, is so immense, so beyond definitions, that calling it God causes a kind of protection against the unknown. After all, even the Bible says, "It is a fearful thing to fall into the hands of the living God." (Hebrews 10:31) If we call the enchanting wonder and source of all life by a name we can comprehend, perhaps then we can control it and control life. We humans like control, or shall I say, the illusion of control.[5]

"Mystery is not to be solved, or resolved, or dissolved. Mystery is to be embraced, loved and out of that will comes one's deepest sense of life, meaning and purpose".[6]

Gilles Quispel

The recovery of enchantment is a recovery of wonder. As any child can live in a world filled with mystery, so each adult has the potential to reclaim that sense of wonder. Inside each of us is that child, who is far older than our adult awareness in many ways. Perhaps this is the meaning behind St. Paul's phrase, "When I was a child, I spoke like a child, I thought like a child, I reasoned like a child; when I became an adult, I put an end to childish ways." (1 Corinthians 13:11) Often we have read that passage as dismissive of the childish view of the world. Could it be suggesting the wisdom of the childlike perspective? After all, that quote is from the famous passage on love in 1 Corinthians 13. "Love is patient; love is kind."

---

[5] I commend the book *What We Talk about When We Talk about God* by Rob Bell. In an accessible read, Bell, a former preacher, describes the various uses of the word God. His approach leaves the reader with an expansive understanding of divinity.

[6] Quispel, https://speakingofjung.com/podcast/2016/4/16/episode-16-russ-lockhart

The challenge we face in midlife is reconnecting and recovering a sense of that wonder, mystery, and indeed enchantment. These are gifts that nourish our soul. Jesus makes forty-nine different references to children in Luke's gospel alone. While our tendency in Western thought is to literalize these teachings, I can't help but wonder if Jesus is talking about something more profound than simply having a children's message just before the adult sermon. Could he be suggesting that while we remain adults with adult intellectual capacity, there still might be something, dare I say magical or enchanting, in the mind of a child?

> People were bringing even infants to him that he might touch them, and when the disciples saw it, they sternly ordered them not to do it. But Jesus called for them and said, "Let the children come to me, and do not stop them, for it is to such as these that the kingdom of God belongs. Truly I tell you, whoever does not receive the kingdom of God as a little child will never enter it." (Luke 18:15-17)

Entering the Kingdom of God may require a beginner's mind, to use a Zen phrase. By this, I mean adopting an attitude of curiosity and inquisitiveness. I recall my time as an environmental education instructor leading elementary school students into the forest for class. Inevitably some children immersed themselves in the experience of crawling under logs with magnifying glasses to experience the wonder of a small square foot of God's kingdom. They articulated with great enthusiasm the wonders of the forest ecosystem. "Wow!" "Hey, look what I found!" "Quick, everyone come see!" That's a beginner's mind, a childlike curiosity that Jesus is welcoming in that passage from Luke's gospel.

But let's be honest, what adult wants to go back to being a child? We have no interest, desire, or capacity to return to that age of innocence. But we yearn to reengage with wonder and grow a sense of delight and enchantment in the world around us. We do this by developing a muscle that once was strong and can be again. That is a muscle of metaphorical sensibility. Cultivate an ability to think symbolically and make use of metaphors. We can still use our deductive reasoning because that's necessary for living in a modern world of cars, commerce, and coffee. Think of this as using both hands to embrace life in the second half. One hand is logical, productive, and planning-oriented, while the other embraces wonder, symbolic thinking, and mystery. You need both hands to grab life. One might be a bit stronger than the other. That's OK. We need some exercise in the realm of enchantment.

Adults Embracing Enchantment.

I'm about to make a shift here. In the first part of this chapter, I introduced you to the idea of enchantment as a critical value in navigating the wisdom needed for the second half of life. In this second section, I will introduce you to some of the Weird Wisdom of enchantment. I want to expose you to two components of the enchanted life: synchronicity and dreams. If you make it through these sections with a heightened degree of curiosity about living an enchanted life, I'll be pleased. More importantly, I think your life will become richer. Additionally, you'll be invited into a new support group I'm starting called "Adults Embracing Enchantment." Maybe we need T-shirts.

In his book *Revelations of Chance: Synchronicity as Spiritual Experience*, Roderick Main highlights a few real-life experiences that serve as examples of enchantment.

The first involves a professor of biology, Adolf Portmann, who, while delivering a lecture, was about to include a story about a praying mantis. Just as he came to the portion of his speech that had the story, a praying mantis flew into the lecture hall and landed on a lectern lamp, thus casting an enormous shadow on the wall in the form of the arms of a praying human being. The second involves the writer Paul Auster who relates that he has had four flat tires in his years of driving.

Spread out over nine years, each flat occurred in a different country and to a different automobile. In each flat tire occurrence, Mr. Auster was accompanied by the same person — an acquaintance he rarely saw. He described his relationship with this person as "always an edge of unease and conflict."[7] A third involves the Swiss psychologist Carl Jung, treating a woman who brought a dream to him. As the woman described the dream and its chief feature of a brooch that looked like a golden scarab, a tapping sound came at the window of Jung's study. He arose and went to the window which he opened and snatched a beetle "whose gold-green color most nearly resembles that of a gold scarab." Jung then, matter-of-factly, handed the beetle to the patient and said, "Here is your scarab."[8]

Another example from my own experience occurred in preparing for this chapter. I had been struggling with a way to approach this section on enchantment. Roderick's book had arrived from the library the day before, but I had not yet opened it. On Saturday morning, I turned on the television to ascertain whether or not our cable lineup of TV stations included one particular channel, in anticipation of an upcoming football game. During my search through the 537 channels available on our cable service, I stumbled across a concert by Yes, the British rock group. I had been a big fan in my youth and chose to watch this concert for about half an hour. I recalled many shows and fan activities with my friends during the 1970s. This is a highly unusual activity for me as I rarely watch television except for occasional sports events. My mind wandered during the concert playing on the screen to the time I visited the site of the Yes Tor, a well-known rock cropping in a park in southwestern England. The band took a photograph for the *Tormato* album cover. My brother and I included a visit during our 1979 backpacking trip across Europe.

---

[7] Main, *Revelations of Chance: Synchronicity as Spiritual Experience*, 15.
[8] Ibid, 1 & 15

After the televised concert concluded, I turned to Roderick's book to begin reading. When I reached page 12, I read a story of a British school teacher, Stephen Jenkins, which described an equally enchanting tale like the ones I mentioned above. The story narrated his visit to a nearby nature park with students. "Jenkins relates that he was on Okehampton Common in Devon, near Yes Tor, where he had gone with a group of school pupils."[9] The phrase Yes Tor leaped off the page at me. This was the same Yes Tor I recalled only thirty minutes earlier while watching the concert footage. I had been a Yes fan years earlier, but I lost interest in the past forty years. So how is it possible that this series of "coincidences" could occur together on that Saturday morning? The events connected the TV concert to a band to a site visited in England in 1979 to a paragraph describing synchronous events. This seemed more than a simple coincidence.

While my example is perhaps not nearly as revelatory as the others, it does serve as a small window into a realm of mystery and enchantment that may be more common in our lives than we currently acknowledge.

Many late-modern people express a profound desire for enchantment. We seem lost without it. I am fully aware of the statistics of the decline in attendance of churches and synagogues and temples across America. But other data points suggest we are hungrier than ever for an encounter with the sacred, the holy, the numinous, or enchantment. As I mentioned in my previous book, *Everyday Spirituality*, there are two familiar places where people describe their experience of the presence of the divine. One is during times of grief, and the other is in the natural world. Belden Lane, author and professor of theology and spirituality, believes those two themes come together in our time.

Increasingly, we are aware of the vulnerability of natural ecosystems. That awareness is revealing a profound grief in the loss of habitat, species,

---

[9] Ibid, 12.

and whole ecosystems. Lane suggests that our grief and vulnerability are growing our understanding of the connectedness of all of nature. This opens late-modern people to seek refuge in the natural world. There is a small but growing interest in alternative spiritualities that profess deeper roots in the natural environment. This occasionally causes controversy among some in traditional expressions of religion, particularly in Christianity. I've witnessed a few angst-ridden communications as news breaks that a minister expresses interest via social media in nature worship, Wiccan rituals, or a revival of Earth Mother spirituality. While I recognize the concerns, I find myself sympathetic to the call of the natural world, God's ongoing Creation. There is a theological and spiritual embrace of nature within Christianity. We just need to mine the resources that have been there all along. They were buried by centuries of fear, but in our time, we can resurrect them. Belden Lane, Larry Rasmussen, and Cynthia Moe-Lobeda are examples of contemporary authors within the Christian ethos who are researching and revealing these traditions.

Many people find enchantment something quite accessible while in nature. And well they should, for the connections in our bodies and religious practices date back hundreds of thousands of years to events in the natural world.

But we are long overdue in this chapter for a story, an ancient story that delights us in our wonderings and wanderings around enchantment. This ancient story comes from Zhuang Zhou, a fourth-century BCE Taoist sage.

One spring, as peach blossoms filled the valley below with a spray of white fragrance, an ancient sage wandered the heights of Shang. He noticed a massive tree on a hillside where all other trees had been chopped down to build a palace for the emperor. This remaining tree was so enormous that the horses drawing a hundred chariots could be sheltered under its shade. It was amazing that it had never been felled. He marveled at how much timber it must contain.

But as he looked up into its branches, he noticed how they were all twisted and crooked, growing in every direction. None were straight enough to be cut into rafters or beams. He broke off a twig and tasted the sap, finding it bitter. The tree would be useless for tapping, producing no syrup of any worth. The leaves, as he crumpled them, gave off an offensive odor. They broke too easily to be woven into mats or braided into baskets. They wouldn't even make good mulch. The roots, moreover, were so gnarled that you'd never be able to carve a bowl or fashion a fine decorative box out of them.

"This indeed," said Zhuang Zhou, "is a tree good for nothing! That's why it has reached such a great old age. The cinnamon tree can be eaten, so it is cut down. The varnish tree is useful and, therefore, incisions are made in it. We all know the advantage of being useful, but only this tree knows the advantage of being useless!"

The Taoist master sat in the shade of the great tree for the rest of the day, as a light wind drifted up from the valley below. He breathed the scent of distant peach blossoms and sat in studied silence, contemplating his own uselessness. He stopped making judgments about the tree's worth, its market value. He sat instead in its welcoming shadow, realizing that his own worth had nothing to do with what he was able to produce.[10]

This is a particularly appropriate story for our purposes. The worth of the tree is not measured by its economic value. This story provides a clear contrast between the material worldview that has come to dominate our lives against a worldview emphasizing stillness and presence. Our society is built on a utilitarian approach to the world, even the natural

---

[10] Lane, *The Great Conversation*, 96. Adapted from James Legge *The Texts of Taoism* (Oxford: Oxford University Press, 1891), book 4, number 7. 6

world. We ask how this wood, river, or species can be used to improve humans' material well-being. Yet this was an ancient sage. Did you catch that phrase at the beginning of the story? Yup, an older person, open to the weird wisdom that can be gained in the second half of life, eventually realized the lesson and sat under the tree. I'm particularly fond of this story because the ancient sage is not portrayed as wise from the beginning. He matures in wisdom through the stages of life. But as time goes by and the sage is willing to sit with the tree, the wisdom comes through.

Money and possessions do not measure worth. This tale reminds us of the inherent worth of each of us, like that of the tree. It's a delightful tale of grace.

Let's get concrete. Here's an example of what I mean by learning to live with enchantment. A while back I was visiting with some friends. We were together for about a week, and as can be the case with close friends, I began to have this experience of an internal voice of judgment emerging. Granted, this voice inside is often with us for various reasons. I love these people dearly and have treasured our relationships over many years, yet those little things they did or said began to irk me. I found myself increasingly possessed by an attitude dominated by judgment. I started thinking critical thoughts more and more. Then one morning, the following happened to me.

As I emerged from a freshwater pond after a good long swim, I picked up the towel and began to dry myself off when I felt a sharp pain in my index finger. I let out a loud "Ouch," followed by a series of expletives. When I examined my finger, I found the remains of a stinger. I concluded I'd been stung by a bee or wasp but could not find the offending insect. I quickly and easily removed the stinger. Since I am not prone to a severe reaction to stings, I went about my day with a mild response and only a tiny bit of swelling.

But the event caused me to reflect on the other times I'd been stung or bitten by an insect. Each time connected with a point of transition in my life. A bee sting on my foot while leading a group of kids as a summer camp counselor occurred during a reevaluation of my career plans. A horse fly inflicted a painful bite while I was on a backpacking trip, recovering from a divorce. A third sting occurred during the COVID-19 pandemic while working in a newly planted garden. All the other times I'd been stung, I found myself at transition points in my life: career changes, relationships ending, or new endeavors about to begin. "Why now?" I wondered. "What might be shifting in me or the world around me that would cause a bee sting?" Now at this point, you might be thinking, look, this is just a random event, Jim. You got stung by a bee. It happens. Move on. Yes, that's one response, but increasingly as I move into the second half of life more fully, I'm curious about the world of nature and the world of meaning. Do those worlds interact? Is there meaning in these events?

My reflection on this particular bee sting began to center on the location of the sting. I suspect the offending creature had found a home inside my folded towel, and when I picked it up, I disturbed it. The sting happened on my index finger, my pointing finger. You'll recall I had fallen into an attitude of judgementalism. The pointing of a finger often is a gesture we use in the act of criticism, chastisement, or judgment. So go ahead right now, make that gesture with your hand and finger: "You are so _____," as you imagine pointing at someone. As I realized this, I also recalled that the pointing hand that includes three fingers pointing back at you.

Jesus had a phrase about seeing sticks in other people while the log is in our own eyes. Then I wondered if the sting of judgment on my pointing judgment finger could be connected to my critical thoughts of my friends. This thought stayed with me in the days that followed, but more importantly, my attitude of judgment against my comrades dissipated. It was as if in this holy moment, nature had conspired to teach me a lesson.

This illustration of nature and meaning crossing paths describes a direction of enchantment worth cultivating as we age.

Dreams: The Royal Road to Enchantment

"If we pay attention to our dreams, instead of living in a cold, impersonal world of meaningless chance, we may begin to emerge into a world of our own, full of important and secretly ordered events."[11] Marie-Louise von Franz

I know of no better way to enchant life than through that magical mystery tour through the world of our dreams. Those peculiar narratives of images emerge each night as we sleep. Dreams are related to the "unfinished business" of waking life. The thoughts, images, and emotions not expressed during the day often appear in our dreams. They are spontaneous self-portraits, only in symbolic form. These night visions emerge from our unconscious and appear in the typical person every night between three and five times. Don't worry; most people don't recall every dream every night, but about three-quarters of people remember dreams from time to time.[12]

Dreams are symbolic stories and images. They are not rational thoughts. I made this mistake once when I dreamed of a shiny new car. I thought this meant I should go out and buy one. But, unfortunately, when the car appeared in our driveway, it didn't land well in our house.[13]

Instead, dreams speak in a language that is filled with both our unrealized potential and our less desirable shadow side. The dream is

---

[11] Von Franz in Jung, *Man and His Symbols*, 208.
[12] Bulkeley, *An Introduction to the Psychology of Dreaming*.
[13] Hazelwood, *Everyday Spirituality: Discover a Life of Hope, Peace and Meaning*, 94-95.

a method for bringing unconscious material into consciousness, whether it came from the outside (something we never became fully aware of) or whether it came totally from the unconscious.[14]

Once a month, I gather a small group of dream sojourners via Zoom. This dream circle engages in a practice of sharing a dream and then exploring its symbolism together. We use the dream projection technique designed by Jeremy Taylor and Robert Haden[15], though there are many quite similar patterns. If we were to attempt to source the original author of this practice, we'd likely spend a lifetime searching. I suspect she lived thousands of years ago. In truth, human beings have been exploring their dreams for 10,000 years or more. Some researchers believe that religion and ritual first emerged in our ancient ancestors as they shared their dreams around campfires. Indigenous people telling of dream encounters with loved ones who had died likely led to early concepts of an afterlife. The first worship services could have involved dance rituals in the reenactment of dreams. Our monthly Dream Circle chooses a much more modest approach as we gather around the glow of our computer screens rather than the glow of a fire.

Recently a member of our dream circle offered the following dream.[16]

> *I am underwater in a vast ocean. There is no vegetation, just a huge ocean. I see a man with long brown hair swimming gracefully, beautifully, like a dancer. The man resembles a teacher of yoga whom I know. He is only wearing a woman's slip that is the same color as his skin. As I watch his beautiful, graceful moves, I hear a voice call out and say, "Agape."*

Is this not a brief and elegant dream capturing a glimpse of a reenchanted world? As our group discussed the dream, we noted many

---

[14] Hoss, *The Psychology of Dreaming*, 7.
[15] Taylor, *Dream Projection Technique*, http://www.thresholdguidance.com/?page_id=254
[16] I am grateful to Gail from our group, who granted permission me to share her dream in this book.

aspects that suggest images and sacredness. Most obviously is hearing the voice say the word *agape*. This ancient Greek word translates as unconditional love, complete and total embrace, and acceptance, typically from God to humans, though it has applications between people. Each time I think of this dream, even though it was not my own, I find myself immersed in a warmth that is reassuring at a level of profound significance.

Dreams are our first language. In evolutionary terms, our ancestors dreamt before they could speak.[17] Dream appreciation means befriending an ancient innate ability in all of us. It is about reclaiming a forgotten language or way of thinking. It means reconnecting with our imaginal mind using symbols and metaphors. In dreams, people and characters are also a metaphor. I like to think of the dream world as an ecosystem filled with a rich biodiversity of imaginings. The whole realm is enchanting, magical, and sometimes bizarre, maybe even frightening. You'll note I'm using the phrase dream appreciation instead of dream interpretation.[18] I prefer this language because our focus here in this adventure of weird wisdom is to engage and appreciate the enchanting world of dreams.

Dream appreciation involves recalling, recording, engaging, and even playing with the dream to explore its meaning and sometimes resolutions to conflicts. These steps can bring positive outcomes in personality change and spiritual growth. Dream appreciation is for everyone. It is a language we can all cherish, like a work of art. Dream interpretation is more specialized and technical. Therefore, dream appreciation consists of practices rather than techniques. Dream appreciation holds that the ultimate interpreter of one's dreams is the dreamer. The dreamer is the expert. Anyone can exercise dream appreciation: a friend, a parent, a co-worker, a community organizer, a church leader.[19]

---

[17] Bulkeley, *Dreaming in the World's Religions*,

[18] William R. Stimson, "Montague Ullman's Dream Appreciation," *The Humanistic Psychologist*, 41:2, 178-198.

[19] Marchiano, This Jungian Life website.

I have found the work of Robert A. Johnson to be particularly helpful in understanding dreams. He outlines a simple yet profound approach in his book *Inner Work: Using Dreams and Active Imagination for Personal Growth*. Johnson's four-step process includes: 1. Making associations; 2. Connecting dream images to inner dynamics; 3. Interpreting; 4. Doing rituals to make the dream concrete.

You'll note that Johnson favors the dreamer as the one interpreting the dream. This is a crucial aspect of dream work. The notion of a book or a website where you plug in your dreams, and a series of answers or equations inform you of what the dream means, is just plain wrong. It's also impossible for another person to tell you what your dream means. Even the most seasoned analysts can only provide you with possible directions for understanding your dreams. While they have much insight, training, and understanding of dreams and symbolic thinking, in the end, they are not the dreamer.

I recall my entrance interview for a training program where I was asked to share a dream. In front of six different trained analysts, I received six different directions to take my dream understanding. Upon reporting this to my analyst, he cited an old apocryphal story from the Jewish Midrash where a man has a profound dream and decides to travel to Jerusalem where he speaks with twenty different rabbis, who all have different interpretations of his dream. The story ends with the man reporting upon his return home, and the peculiar thing was, all twenty interpretations were true. Here we have the multi-variegated and enchanting world of dreams.

This is why I emphasize dream appreciation instead of interpretation in my work of spiritual direction and dream circles. I want us to swim in the dream and thereby pursue the weird wisdom of enchantment. I'll leave interpretation up to those professionals trained in that field. For our pursuit of reenchanting life, let's rest in the experience of the dream. Using the example of Gail's dream, it's perhaps appropriate to imagine the experience of floating in the water, watching the man with Jesus-like long hair, and hearing the word *agape* echo through our souls. Pause for a moment and slow down enough to take in all that imagery and absorb the wonder of it all. Our souls will know what to do with that. There is no need to over-intellectualize what this might mean. The unconscious is communicating, and maybe it's just best to let the ego step back and allow for our whole being to experience this *agape* dream. Our goal is to live a reenchanted life.

David Tacey has written a book titled *The Post-Secular Sacred*.[20] His thesis is that we have gone through a time since the Enlightenment that has resulted in a secular worldview. While necessary and helpful for us as a species, we took the movement too far and killed the sacred. The idea of a world without religion, without spirit, without wonder held the promise of a world of apparent rationality and human progress. The hoped-for secular world didn't exactly turn out all that great. What's emerging now is a revival of the sacred. As I've mentioned here, we are seeing interest in a diversity of interests in spirituality. Indeed, it's the re-enchantment of the world that is capturing our attention. Those seeking the weird wisdom to help navigate the second half of life find enchantment a resource they cannot do without.

Retired Methodist minister Jim Warner, now deceased, served alongside both my wife and me while we were parish pastors. I recall a piece of wisdom he shared with me. "I used to think that the older I got, the clearer life's meaning would be to me. But instead, I'm finding it all becoming less clear, more mysterious. I have more questions now than in the past." Most of us in the second half of life find that to be true. It's kind of weird. But embracing that perspective rather than running from it will serve us well in these years.

---

[20] Tacey, *The Post-Secular Sacred.*

Chapter 5

Integrity

I've learned that people will forget what you said, people will forget what you did, but people will never forget how you made them feel.

—*Maya Angelou*

We live in the age of the pursuit of integrity. Everywhere I turn, I hear of people's desire for authenticity, transparency, and integrity. Yet, as trust in institutions and leaders eroded over the past fifty years, our cynicism rose. At the same time, our hunger for genuine, ethical, and mature people has grown. We long for people who demonstrate a combination of care and clarity. The second half of life is an opportunity to become one of those people. To be the change we long to see in the world, to paraphrase Gandhi.[1]

My first introduction to integrity came via a mini-scandal when I was 15 years old. My family immersed itself in the youth soccer movement of the 1970s, where every Saturday, the fields of Balboa Park in southern California filled with hundreds of kids playing soccer. My mother coached, my youngest brother played, and my father refereed, later becoming the director of about sixty referees. He coordinated, scheduled, trained, and supervised a motley crew of people aged 15 to 65 who served as the umpires. That motley crew of referees included one skinny, long-haired teenager, namely me.

---

[1] Gandhi, *The Story of My Experiments with Truth*, 70. The exact quote reads as follows: "As human beings, our greatness lies not so much in being able to remake the world as in being able to remake ourselves. The change that we are looking for has to be in the individual, not in the social order. The individual has to be the change he or she wants to see in the world."

One late fall afternoon, I officiated a game between two talented teams. During play, I whistled a foul near the goal and awarded a penalty kick. The coach from the defending team exploded in a sideline rage that required several parents to prevent him from physically charging me on the field. Not interested in continuing under those circumstances, I suspended the game and walked off the field.

Little did I know that the events of this game would become quite the topic of conversation for several weeks. My father no doubt received numerous complaints. Finally, before the monthly meeting of all the referees, my dad spoke to me privately at our home. Calmly and clearly, he asked me to describe what happened on the field and after the game. I told him what I saw, the foul I called, and the events around suspending the game. He responded by explaining that a foul in the penalty area should be blatant, bordering on intentional, because "we as referees don't want to be making calls that potentially influence the outcome of the game." In other words, based on what I described, he determined I'd likely made a poor decision.

That evening at the monthly meeting, as my father conducted business, one of the referees (I later learned a friend of the grieved coach) stood and spoke critically of how the game had been officiated. My father responded calmly and clearly that "we as referees have a difficult task, but no matter what happens, we as a group stand together. We don't turn on each other." On the way home, I remained quiet, as did he. Eventually, we pulled into the driveway. I finally broke the silence and said, "Thank you." He responded, "You're welcome."

We never spoke of that incident again. My father and I had an awkward relationship. Our introverted personalities made communication difficult. When he died in 2005 at the age of 78, I spoke briefly at his funeral and told the above story. All these years later, I have three or four significant memories of my relationship with my father, some good, some not so good. This event stands out as my lesson on the power of integrity.

Years later, I worked as a summer camp counselor between college semesters. Somehow, I got pulled into a discussion by the two directors about the camp cook. Someone had complained about the behavior of the cook's five-year-old daughter. One of the directors wanted to have an all-staff meeting, make a public apology, and write a letter to the constituent membership. Though only 22 at the time, I interrupted this discussion with an emphatic, "No. That's not what we should do. We should deal with this internally one on one, but our public face is one of support of our staff." I had no idea where that statement came from until I assembled items for this book and realized its roots. To this day, in my dealings as a leader, I have attempted to live out the lesson my father modeled for me. Criticize privately, support publicly. My record on this is not perfect by any means, but it remains a true north conviction for me.

Integrity is one of the values we seek to reclaim in our years after the midpoint. When we make the turn from those decades of establishing ourselves, our careers, our families, as well as strengthening our egos and building confidence, we inevitably turn back and reflect. When we do that, we recall mistakes, blunders, failures. A whole series of regrets come to mind. So how do we reintegrate those losses into our lives?

Integrity is a word rooted in the Latin word *integer*, first known in the 14th century, meaning "entire." This word contains the prefixes "in" and "tag," which are the roots of the words entire and integrity, as well as the mathematical term we use today denoting a whole number. All these meanings yielded not just "integrity" but also "integral," meaning "to make whole."[2] Indeed, the process of seeking integrity is about making ourselves, our relationships, and our world whole. To arrive at that ever-elusive state of wholeness, we integrate aspects of our past.

---

[2] Ayto, *Dictionary of Word Origins*, 203.

In this chapter, I want to explore integrity from two perspectives. The first is how we understand integrity in our tangible outward actions and behaviors. The second is in that more personal zone of our inner landscapes. While both are profoundly connected, it might be easier to explore them separately before bringing them together.

Let's tackle the first aspect of integrity as we consider it as an outward manifestation of our lives. An old Zen story would be helpful right about now. This is an early story titled "Is That So?" from the Zen Buddhist tradition, likely originating in Japan.

> The Zen Master Hakuin was praised by his neighbors as one living a pure life. At one time, a beautiful young Japanese woman, whose parents owned a food store, lived near him. Suddenly, without any warning, her parents discovered she was with child. This made her parents angry. She would not confess who the man was, but after much harassment, she named Hakuin.
>
> In great anger, the parents went to the master. "Is that so?" was all he would say.
>
> After the child was born, it was brought to Hakuin. He had lost his reputation by this time, which did not trouble him, but he took very good care of the child. He obtained milk from his neighbors and everything else the little one needed.
>
> A year later, the young woman-mother could stand it no longer. She told her parents the truth — that the child's birth father was a young man who worked in the fish market. The mother and father of the young woman at once went to Hakuin to ask his forgiveness, to apologize at length, and to get the child back again. Hakuin was willing. In yielding the child, all he said was: "Is that so?"[3]

---

[3] Reps, *Zen Flesh Zen Bones: A Collection of Zen and Pre-Zen Writings*, 22. Note: I have left this telling intact but amended the language of the 1957 translation from the word girl to young woman. This updates the language that reflects our current understanding of the way we refer to women of childbearing age.

Who among us could respond to such an event in the manner of Hakuin? I would be hard-pressed not to jump to my feet and start shouting, "Hey, wait a minute. That's not me. I don't even know this person." I'd be highly defensive. Unlike Hakuin, I would be concerned about my reputation. After all, my integrity is at stake. Besides, if something similar were to unfold today, imagine the headlines and social media fiasco that would develop.

We expend a great deal of energy maintaining our public faces to the world. Whether we are public figures, leaders, students, or parents, this is true. We have a great deal invested in our reputations. Carl Jung described this as our persona, the "I" that we present to the world. "Originally, the word persona meant a mask worn by actors to indicate the role they played. On this level, it is both a protective covering and an asset in mixing with other people. Civilized society depends on interactions between people through the persona."[4] In short, our persona is the public face we present to the world, and it's needed because it helps us function in the world of mortgages, meals, and mosquitos. As we move through life, we connect it to our inner self. But more on that in a moment. For now, we are still investigating integrity in our outer existence.

As the years go by, I place a higher and higher value on my integrity as a person, bishop, parent, and grandparent. Yes, I've heard people say, "The older I get, the less I care what people think of me." I'm hopeful that means they are less tied to other people's opinions outwardly influencing them. As I get older, I may care less about the frivolous such as what people think of my weight, attire, or hairstyle. But I am committed to the values I communicate to people. Am I fair, just, and ethical in my decision-making? Do I have a reputation as a listener, or am I just another bloviator? Will my son feel comfortable coming to me when he is in a crisis? Do people see me as wise or run the other way

---

[4] Sharp, Jungian Lexicon https://www.psychceu.com/Jung/sharplexicon.html

because I'm pompous and ignorant? These are the questions that matter to me.

The author David Brooks articulated this well in a 2015 column when he wrote about the contrast between the resumé virtues and the eulogy virtues.[5] The resumé virtues are the kind of stuff we hear about constantly in our culture. Hardworking, productive, efficient are the highlights of the resumé list, and likely those are the first half of life virtues. The eulogy virtues are those qualities we hope people will say about us at our funerals. Were you kind, brave, honest, and faithful? That's what we hope our friends and family will say about us when six strong men and women carry us to the cemetery.

How do we get to that place where people speak of us in glowing but honest terms? I once heard a granddaughter read the passage from 1 Corinthians 13 at her grandfather's funeral. It's typically read at weddings, and because I've listened to it read hundreds of times in that context, the words had become light, fluffy, and meaningless to me. I had witnessed so many marital conflicts and divorces that this overly idealistic portrait of love at a wedding made me cynical. (Not a virtue I want to be known for, alas, I have work to do.) But when a teenage woman who treasured her grandfather opened his Bible and read St. Paul's words of love, I was utterly astounded.

> What if I could speak
> all languages
> of humans
>   and of angels?
> If I did not love others,
>   I would be nothing more
> than a noisy gong
>   or a clanging cymbal.

---

[5] Brooks, "The Moral Bucket List" *New York Times*, April 2015.

² What if I could prophesy
and understand all secrets
   and all knowledge?
And what if I had faith
   that moved mountains?
I would be nothing,
   unless I loved others.
³ What if I gave away all
   that I owned
and let myself
   be burned alive?
I would gain nothing,
   unless I loved others.
⁴ Love is kind and patient,
never jealous, boastful,
   proud, or ⁵ rude.
Love isn't selfish
   or quick-tempered.
It doesn't keep a record
   of wrongs that others do.
⁶ Love rejoices in the truth,
   but not in evil.
⁷ Love is always supportive,
loyal, hopeful,
   and trusting.
⁸ Love never fails! (1 Corinthians 13:1-8 CEV)

She was articulating in words all that she saw in her grandfather. "If I did not love others, I would be nothing more than a noisy gong." I wonder whether my grandsons will offer to read something so powerful at my memorial.

These questions begin to dominate our thinking in the second half of life. How will I be remembered? Who will miss me and why? What virtues will be highlighted at my funeral?

We'll come back to this again in the last chapter, but for now, let's recognize that an outward concern for our integrity looms large in our souls as we move through the years.

A significant step toward a life worth living must also concern our inner integrity. How do we integrate those regrets, mistakes, and disappointments? Before we look at the "how," let's explore why this is an essential part of the second half of life.

Let's borrow from the work of James Hollis, who uses the metaphor of a haunted house. In his book *Living an Examined Life*, Hollis suggests that we all live in a haunted house. No, he's not referring to that place down the street at Halloween. Instead, he's using the image of a haunted house to describe our inner life. We carry plenty of memories, wounds, regrets that seem to occupy various places in our internal home. Hollis suggests that our greatest challenge is the specter of an unlived life. He challenges us, "If we live in haunted houses, we are called to turn the lights on and clean house."[5]

The hauntings that demand integration in the second half of life vary from person to person. We all have them. They include experiences within our own families as well as how society defines us as a boy or girl, a man or woman. These alone had a major impact as we grew up. Women often tell me of the constraints and limitations placed on them throughout their lives. Men are more cautious about opening up about their experiences, mainly because we felt shame around expressing our vulnerabilities early in life. Almost every child has a period early on when they leave behind the joy, spontaneity, creativity, and enthusiasm of early childhood. The boy or girl may walk away from that early life due to social conditions such as poverty, racial profiling, lack of education, or other constricting conditions. Even those who grew up in relatively healthy and mature families can recall experiences of poor role models, bad theology, ignorant caregivers, or just plain less than

---

[5] Hollis, *Living an Examined Life*, 86.

ideal circumstances. These hauntings are within us, and the second half of life requires us to turn on the lights. This is the internal work of integrity through integration.

Why do this inner work? The short answer is that a meaningful life calls us to this work. Some of us have no choice; we know deep down that there is a path toward finding purpose and meaning in life. That path leads into the hauntings of our souls. Engaging in a conversation with the deeper parts of our souls brings greater purpose, dignity, and meaning to this journey we call life.

Cathy initially thought this path of examining her inner life was ridiculous. "I'm quite content with my life and my faith as it is, thank you very much," she told a group of adults in a book discussion group I led. Yet, in the months that unfolded, Cathy began to experience a series of uncomfortable thoughts stimulated mainly by both the books we were reading and the conversations in our group. I thought she would leave the group and walk away from the church for a while. But slowly, I noticed her articulating questions that suggested she was moving in a different direction. After one session, she shared a dream of an older man inviting her into an old house that resembled her childhood home. He stood with her on the porch and gestured for her to enter the front door. In the dream, she says, "I'm afraid," to which the old man (often a symbol of a wisdom figure) responded, "I'll go with you."

I suggested Cathy begin seeing a friend who provides spiritual direction and therapy depending on the need. Her response is indicative of many people's thoughts. "Do you think I'm mentally ill?" "No." I boldly proclaimed. "I want you to see John, whom I know and trust because you have been given this great gift. This dream is a calling to examine your life. A therapist in the Jungian tradition is there to help you, walk with you, guide you as you learn. Cathy, this is a wonderful opportunity for you to grow deeper, find more meaning and purpose."

She and I engaged in a lively exchange. I'd known her for a long time, and we were comfortable speaking freely with one another. Her feisty streak intimidated many people, but I learned to engage her rather than run from her. Eventually, after many conversations, she opted to try it.

Years later, Cathy told me how grateful she began that work long ago. "I've learned so much about myself," she reports. "But you need to know, I was pretty pissed off at you for a while." She was referencing a time when she began to lose her faith as a Christian. The positive attitude to her friends at church began to erode. People noticed, she noticed, and it caused her to step away from some commitments for a period. Changes shifted in her marriage as well. But over time, a resilience and a deepening of interests developed in her. Today she continues in her church, but instead of serving in more traditional roles for a woman, she stepped into leadership capacities and started a women's Bible study at a nearby prison. "I never would have done those things without this group. You all helped me investigate places that I had never examined. I'm a stronger and healthier person because of it. My husband thinks so too." Cathy is an example of why this integration work is essential and rewarding.

To be a person of integrity requires integration. Remember our description of the origins of the word. It's connected with integers, and wholeness. A person of integrity has integrated multiple aspects of their life. We've all spent the first half of life building up a portfolio of work, family, and personality. But as we did that, we made choices along the way, or perhaps choices were made for us. This means we left some attributes behind.

Regrets and disappointments are natural parts of our lives, and arriving at midlife with an accumulation of aspects of an unlived life is universal. Those can include jobs not taken, relationships not pursued, opportunities lost. But they can also include a sense of humor stifled, artistic inclinations rejected, or fears that overwhelmed us. To live a life as long as you've lived and not have regrets, wounds, or disappointment would not be typical. The well-known slogan "No Regrets" may sound appealing, but it likely reflects an attitude that is, well, just not human.

Where have all those left-behind tasks, thoughts, or emotions gone? Did they just disappear? Unlikely. More than likely, they are rattling around in the basements of our souls. If we are to be people of integrity, it may be time to integrate those hauntings, bring them up to the main floor. Most of us will need help doing this work. I don't necessarily mean professional help, but we will need a partner or two or seven. People who love us, accept us, encourage us. Friends, co-workers, ministers, family members, all the folks who people our lives.

The pursuit of integration often involves asking those questions we began asking of ourselves a long time ago:

Who am I?
What is this life all about?
Am I called to something larger than this?
What do I believe, and why?

Those questions can be answered simplistically. I am Jim. Life is about getting more money. I don't want a more meaningful life. Where is the TV remote? I believe in me, myself, and I; nothing more. Those answers are satisfactory, and many people opt for those options or alternatives that include a drink or new clothes, patriotism, acquisition, or gambling. Some people express little desire to go beyond those perspectives. Yet, others know on some level that those questions call for something more.

"Who am I?" is a question that rumbles in our bodies. We respond in significant ways to a film, a piece of art, or a new book. We resonate with a song we hear at church or on the radio. The questions begin to roll through us in new ways. "Who am I?" persistently nags away deep within us, and we can't ignore it. Not only can we not ignore it, but we also hunger to pursue it. We are eager and look for opportunities to probe the question. Then suddenly, while visiting a friend, we see a book on their coffee table with an intriguing title, or we sign up for art classes, or we set out on a road trip with a colleague. It's as if simply holding the question in our minds and bodies begs for a response.

My friend Susan says, "I just put it out to the universe, and an answer comes." Another friend describes the prayer she recites every morning, while a third friend tells me of his musings on the way to work. Whatever the approach, the more profound questions of life get articulated and while the answer may not come instantly, often what happens is that an entry point reveals itself.

Shortly after turning 60, I wondered what happened to the pastorate I was supposed to rebuild. The dream I'd had fifteen years earlier returned to me. You remember, the one I described in the introduction to this book, where the professor walks up to me and says, "It's time to rebuild your pastorate." Wondering about that dream and some of the more fundamental questions of life, I awoke one morning around my sixtieth birthday and recorded the following dream.

> *I am on what seems to be a vacation visiting a city park in Rome. First, I see a few statues and ancient ruins in the park. They are eroded, discolored, and partially covered in vegetation. Then I come across some steps that lead underground below the park. I find a large cavern filled with hundreds and hundreds of people gathered for a worship service. It seems I am the founder of this new church. A man and woman walk up to welcome me, and they say, "This is not a church with answers, though you will find answers along the way."*

Between discussions with a dream exploration group and my spiritual director, and my own pondering of this dream, I wonder if that pastorate I was called to rebuild might be taking the form of a new interior church. The rich symbolism of ancient ruins above ground, and the new sacred space below ground, all seem to suggest an emerging new direction within me. The dramatic quote from the couple in the dream emphasizes something I've highlighted in this book, namely that life unfolds as one discovery after another. In other words, answers are found along the way. Relearning that lesson is a form of integrity for me.

One of my father's habits was to recite poetry he had memorized as a student. I always marveled at this because it was such an unusual practice for a scientist trained in the 1950s. "If," the poem by the 19th century British author Rudyard Kipling, was one of his favorites. Except for the last line, it is just as relevant for women. The poem has stayed with me as a part of his efforts to communicate the importance of integrity.

If

If you can keep your head when all about you
    Are losing theirs and blaming it on you,
If you can trust yourself when all men doubt you,
    But make allowance for their doubting too,
If you can wait and not be tired by waiting,
    Or, being lied about, don't deal in lies,
Or, being hated, don't give way to hating,
    And yet don't look too good, nor talk too wise;

If you can dream—and not make dreams your master,
    If you can think—and not make thoughts your aim,
If you can meet with Triumph and Disaster
    And treat those two impostors just the same,
If you can bear to hear the truth you've spoken
    Twisted by knaves to make a trap for fools,
Or watch the things you gave your life to, broken,
    And stoop and build 'em up with worn out tools;

If you can make one heap of all your winnings
    And risk it on one turn of pitch-and-toss,
And lose, and start again at your beginnings.
    And never breathe a word about your loss,

If you can force your heart and nerve and sinew
    To serve your turn long after they are gone,
And so hold on when there is nothing in you
    Except the Will which says to them: "Hold on"

If you can talk with crowds and keep your virtue,
    Or walk with Kings—nor lose the common touch;
If neither foes nor loving friends can hurt you;
    If all men count with you, but none too much;
If you can fill the unforgiving minute
    With sixty seconds' worth of distance run—
Yours is the Earth and everything that's in it,
    And—which is more—you'll be a Man, my son!

CHAPTER 6

Relationships

Through my research I found that vulnerability is the glue that holds relationships together. It's the magic sauce.[1]

— Brené Brown

The "R" in our Weird Wisdom wordplay stands for relationships—those curious objects of interaction who seem so like us and sometimes just so unlike us. For many, the objects of our engagement are other people but could include a whole variety of creation. We'll get to that later. For now, let's focus on relations we have with the humans who make this same weird journey with us.

Harvard professor Arthur Brooks writes a column for *The Atlantic* magazine on the keys to happiness. According to a Harvard study, the most critical trait of happy, well-adjusted elders is healthy relationships.[2] As Robert Waldinger, who currently directs the study, told Brooks in an email, "Well-being can be *built*—and the best building blocks are good, warm relationships."[3]

Well, there you have it. You can stop reading now. If I'd been more efficient, I could have shortened this book and just referenced that study in the first paragraph of the first page. You could have saved both time and money. But relationships are key.

---

[1] https://www.ted.com/talks/brene_brown_the_power_of_vulnerability?utm_campaign=tedspread&utm_medium=referral&utm_source=tedcomshare

[2] https://news.harvard.edu/gazette/story/2017/04/over-nearly-80-years-harvard-study-has-been-showing-how-to-live-a-healthy-and-happy-life/

[3] https://www.theatlantic.com/family/archive/2022/02/happiness-age-investment/622818/

There is a danger in our focus to this point. Perhaps you've already picked up on a key missing ingredient to the Weird Wisdom approach. One could have read to this point and begun to wonder, is the second half of life purely a solo ride? Are we on our own? Ah, good reader, you are astute. You have detected a vital missing ingredient. It's time we turn to the big "R" of relationships and their role in the wisdom we need for this journey.

Knowing that people have much wisdom regarding relationships, I invited readers of my regular *Substack* newsletter to send me their vignettes, stories, and modern parables of their experience of relationships throughout a lifetime. I naively thought I would receive poetic hallmarks like celebrations and good cheer scenarios: tales of the people who made a difference in their lives, inspiring anecdotes of influential grandparents, and tiny briefs on favorite teachers, pastors, and neighbors. But that's not what happened. Instead, people wrote to me of heartache, loss, and the fracturing of their lives. I received a steady stream of tales of divorce, conflict over religion or politics, children who abandoned their parents, and vice versa. My inbox slowly filled with the narrative that relationships often break apart and break our hearts as we continue through our lives. I began to wonder what wisdom we can gain from these broken experiences. What does this tell us about ourselves and our late-modern world? How can we move through these encounters with loss and grief and mature as people?

> "The truth about intimate relationships is that they can never be any better than our relationship with ourselves ... All relationships, therefore, are symptomatic of the state of our inner life, and no relationship can be better than our relationship to our own unconscious."[4]

---

[4] Hollis, *The Middle Passage: From Misery to Meaning in Mid-Life*, 47.

The first time I read that passage from Jim Hollis, I became exceedingly defensive. Why? It forced me to look at a past marriage of mine. Ten years before, a short-lived marriage fell apart in an amicable divorce of my own initiating. Although I had since remarried, moved across the country, started a new career and family, I still recall the first time I read that passage in Hollis' book, *The Middle Passage.* I reacted with a series of statements that included, *no way, it was not my fault, I was the righteous one, I'm still blaming her,* etc. You get the idea. The book had been suggested to me by an Episcopal priest who was also a Jungian analyst. Two weeks later, I was in his office telling him, with a healthy degree of passion, what I thought of this stupid book and its observations about relationships. After my mini-rant concluded, he simply looked at me and said, "Well, that certainly touched a nerve." I spent the next several years learning and relearning a series of lessons centered around taking responsibility for my part in ending that relationship.

Relationships are hard. They are also richly rewarding, what makes life worth living, an opportunity for joy, and a chance to have a person or small community of people who are witnesses to our lives. But they are also fraught with challenges that demand, well, they demand our very souls. Whether those relationships are with a spouse, a partner, a child, a parent, a co-worker, a friend, we inevitably run up against the slings and arrows of outrageous fortune. Relationships are hard.

Let's get some help understanding the multifaceted nature of relationships from an old story. This is a folk tale called "The Lute Player," originally from Russia. Like many folk tales, various versions of this motif circulate throughout the world, which speaks to a universal or archetypal pattern. I've edited this folk tale for length to bring you to the essence of the story, but you can read the full version along with commentary in a fine book by Allan Chinen.

Once upon a time, a King and Queen lived happily together. One day, the King felt restless and decided to wage war on a heathen lord, infamous for cruelty and evil. Following a ferocious battle, which he lost, the King was captured and thrown into a dungeon. After three years of captivity and misery, the King befriended a guard and penned a letter to his wife, the Queen, imploring her to ransom the entire kingdom and pay for his freedom.

When the Queen read the letter, she wept in distress for the fate of both the King and the realm. Realizing she could not go herself before the heathen lord for fear of being captured, she devised a plan whereby she would cut off her hair, dress as a boy, and bring her lute to buy passage to the heathen lord. She traveled far and wide, playing her lute and singing her songs, eventually outside the evil lord's castle.

Upon hearing the sweet music, the lord invited the marvelous lute player into his palace to perform. "Your music soothes me," said the heathen lord. "Play your lute and sing for me. Stay for three days, and I shall give you your heart's desire." This warlord of the castle became entranced for three days. The Queen, dressed as a boy, stopped on the last day.

"My lord," she said, "I must take my leave. I am a traveler, and the road is my home."

The heathen lord acknowledged his agreement and granted her one wish, her heart's desire. The Queen said, "I travel alone and desire a companion, give me one of your prisoners for company." The lord granted this request, and the lute player chose her husband from among the prisoners. He was now relatively thin and scarred from his ordeal. Upon release, he did not recognize his wife, and she said nothing to him. They traveled together for many miles returning to their own country, and all the while she never revealed her true identity.

Upon their return to their own country, the King proclaimed, "I am the King of this land, and if you release me, I shall reward you greatly." "Go in peace," said the Queen, still dressed as a boy. "I need no reward." The two parted ways, but the Queen knew a shortcut, so she snuck through their castle walls and changed into her royal gown. When the King returned to his chambers and confronted his Queen, he was angry. "Who is this woman who left me to die in prison?" Despite the protestations of his minister's explanation, he cast her off, shouting, "Faithless wife!"

But the Queen returned to her chambers and quickly changed into her traveling cloaks, grabbed her lute, and went outside the castle walls to begin playing and singing songs. Upon hearing the music, the King ran outside, saying, "He is the one who freed me." And taking the lute player's hand, said, "You must tell me your heart's desire, and I shall give it to you."

"I desire only you," said the Queen as she removed her cloaks and revealed herself. The King was stunned for a moment, speechless, and then embraced the Queen, begging her forgiveness and thanking her for rescuing him. He then ordered a double celebration, one for his rescue and one more for the Queen's wisdom.[5]

One of the significant challenges of relationships is that all relationships live in the tension of the desire for intimacy on the one hand and the calling for individual identity on the other hand. How can we be both with and for the other while also claiming our independence? Closeness with another always seems to coexist with intimacy with ourselves. This seems true in a relationship, a work, or the duties and commitments we hold in this world.

This old folk tale reveals much, but let's keep our attention on the King and Queen both as a couple and as individuals. Note how in the beginning, all seems well until the King seems eager for adventure, in this case, war. In our time, that war can be a career or a cause; something appears to possess the man to leave the harmony that seems to be

---

[5] Chinen, Once Upon a Midlife: Classic Stories and Mythic Tales to Illuminate the Middle Years, 74.

available right at home. Clearly, in our 21st century world, we can adjust the genders and witness the woman going off to some pursuit. The point is that in any homeostatic relationship, there often comes the point where one party looks elsewhere for energy, excitement, adventure. There seems to be something built into our relationships with others that make it hard to stay in the tension and hold together.

Because our expectations in marriage put pressure on the partner to fulfill all our needs, the burden can be quite heavy. Ouch! That's a lot to ask of another human being, and frankly, it's not possible. My wife cannot meet all my expectations, nor can I meet all of hers. In my friendships, I consistently encounter limitations. No single friend can be everything I am hoping for in a companion. I have great conversations about matters of significance; in another, I laugh and argue, and we talk shop. We cannot be all things to all people, and we know that. But, equally, we cannot be all things even to a single person.

While the King is in prison, he desperately reaches out to the Queen, who responds not by taking his suggestion, which would impoverish the entire realm, but by tapping into her muse. That muse happens to be music, which she uses as a tool to release her husband from prison. In this way, the Queen has her own adventure as well. This is a necessary act on the part of the woman in this case. She sets out to discover her gifts, and the precipitating event is this plea for help. Yet she has equal concern for both the kingdom as a whole and herself. She is attempting to hold both intimacy and independence together. Not an easy thing to do.

It's intriguing to consider that one of the lessons we learn in the Weird Wisdom of the second half of life centers around creation. I know numerous people who undertook a creative endeavor at some point along the way, be it pottery, gardening, woodworking, or playing a musical instrument like our Queen. The second half of life allows for and invites us to exercise the muse, that creative energy the Greeks attributed to the divine realm. Notice how it is in the exercise of the muse that the

King and Queen are reunited. Does this suggest that the two can be held together when there is a third person or task, rather than expecting everything to be satisfied by the other person? That third can be a host of activities, interests, or even spiritual dimensions. By the way, an archaic meaning of the word muse is related to wonder and marvel.[6]

As is the case with many folk tales, this story contains insights and layers of meaning. I've simply pulled a few hints from this one. Ironically, this tale is originally from Russia. As I write this chapter, modern-day Russia has abandoned the Queen and gone off to war in Ukraine. Here's hoping the muse can bring music to the bear and return peace to the land.

Men and Relationships

One of the more challenging aspects of the second life involves men and our relationships. In American culture, women are often the primary connectors between people. Their internal capacity to connect with others seems natural. Unfortunately, the same is not true for men, especially heterosexual men. We seem challenged to build relationships with others, particularly other men. Earlier in life, we men found opportunities for friendship with comrades through sports, school, military service, and work. But as the years progress, those natural opportunities for male bonding disappear. It's not unusual for a man in his retirement years to have no other male friends in whom he can confide. This has lasting detrimental impacts for men as individuals, as well as for our society in general. James Hollis and Nancy Furlotti have addressed this societal predicament in their short film *Soulheal*.[7] They conclude that many men raised in the modern world are so disconnected

---

[6] Oxford English Dictionary,

[7] https://www.soulhealfilm.com

from the core of emotional and spiritual guidance that we fall prey to the messages of competition, violence, and rage.

Outside of my work life, I have found making friends with other men difficult. And finding another man or two with whom I can speak of my deepest concerns, fears, and personal challenges is nearly impossible. When I tell women this, they are often horrified. "How do you live?" they say. "I'd be dead if I didn't have my walking partners, my book club, or my church friends."

For that reason, in my 50s, I began to intentionally reach out to some guys I had known through the years. I had no illusions of creating something that a woman would find meaningful; I sought to connect with other men in a more traditional masculine way. It began with a reengagement with bicycle riding. As a young boy, I discovered the joy of independence through riding a bike. In my late elementary school years, I joined friends riding around the San Fernando Valley and later spent a summer riding my Schwinn Continental thirteen miles to a job as an assistant to our school custodian. The experience taught me much about navigating traffic, calculating commuting time, and the responsibilities of my first job. I called it my thousand-mile summer as I clocked the miles on an odometer.

When my son and daughter-in-law announced they were pregnant, I realized that meant I'd be a grandfather. The joy and surprise of this news catapulted me into several midlife transitions. This included a desire to take care of my body. Among the many activities I resurrected was my bicycling interest. Thanks to a friend named Bill Bishop, I rediscovered the joy and freedom of cycling.

I reconnected with friends I had met in college. We had worked together as summer camp counselors and environmental education instructors at El Camino Pines, a Lutheran camp and retreat center located in the mountains of the Los Padres National Forest north of Los Angeles. The bond we formed there had a life-changing impact on all of us. Forty years later, residing around the country, we began various summer bicycle excursions. My friend Kurt and I rode across New York State via the Erie Canal, Erik joined us the following May along the coast of North Carolina, Rick and I tackled the hills of Vermont. In the summer of 2019, seven of us gathered for RAGBRAI®, a week-long bicycle ride across the state of Iowa. A few years later, we made the trek down the Oregon coast. Last year we camped and cycled along the Great Allegheny Passage® from Pittsburgh to Washington, DC. The experience of riding and camping together has reestablished our connections. Our text message chain has an activity level that rivals many a teenage group.

In 2020 at the height of the COVID-19 pandemic, we bid farewell to Frank, one of our close friends, who died of cancer at the age of 61. The news provided soberness to our jovial gang. We had lost a contemporary, the first of our group. Frank combined many of the qualities our culture needs in a man. He demonstrated integrity in his work and family life. Weird Wisdom pervaded his spirit, and if he were with us today, he'd also find the humor and tease me mercilessly about my weirdness. A lasting image of our group stems from a visit to the site of the famous *American Gothic* painting by Grant Wood. Frank and I posed as the couple in front of the iconic house in rural Iowa, Frank in the dress and me holding the pitchfork. After Loren grabbed the initial staged photograph, Frank kissed me. Loren snapped the shutter. A brief moment was captured of the King and Queen reunited. We all miss him.

I know of a few other men that have similar patterns. One holds an annual fishing and camping gathering with his brothers. Another man reunites with four friends for a motorcycle trip through various Western states. A third man brings together a few friends for a road trip to a different baseball park each summer. The conversations on these adventures range from the silly to the serious and occasionally include moments, often brief, in which the wounds of loss and disappointment are expressed. Those moments would not occur without the context of the trip. Why? Because men need time with other men to adjust, settle in, slowly watching and testing the safety of the others. The combination of a culturally reinforced pattern of guardedness along with an evolutionary built-in self-preservation gene inhibits our ability to sit down over a meal and "open up."

James Hollis writes: men wonder "Why should I share my weakness, my failure, my vulnerability with someone else? They might use it against me."[8] Along with others such as Harry Willmar M.D., Hollis has written and worked extensively with men in a therapeutic setting. Unfortunately, the vast majority of men are very reluctant to make their way into a therapist's consulting room; most won't go unless the outer world forces them to do so, often via a job loss, a marriage breakup, or a chemical addiction. The idea of going to an analyst or a spiritual director to "work on oneself," grow or heal, sounds ridiculous and a "waste of time" to most men.

As an alternative, men could seek out the companionship I've described. If you are a man reading this section, you know what I'm portraying. I encourage you to find a small group of other men and plan an adventure together. Repeat it as often as possible. You are slowly building the trust and companionship that comes only with time and shared experiences. Gradually you'll discover how important this group is for you. It also might save you from going off to war and ending up imprisoned, as our King found. Had he a group of merry pranksters, teammates, fishing buddies, he might have saved himself some prison time. But then his Queen might not have found her muse.

I'm aware of the women reading this book who might wonder why it is necessary to include a chapter on relationships. The natural response from most women might be, "Well, of course, you need relationships in life, it's not life without them." Women know this, for

---

[8] Hollis, *The Broken Mirror*, 108.

they are relational beings in their very essence. Men are as well, it's just that upbringing, culture, and history have depleted this foundational element of our human experience.

But why do we need relationships? There are many answers, ranging from the drive to bring forth the next generation into the world, to the sheer joy of sharing life's celebrations with another, to the sustenance we need from others in times of great pain. But I would add that we also need relationships to become individuals. "Becoming oneself demands perpetual risk-taking and sacrifice within relationships," writes London-based psychotherapist Martin Schmidt. [9]

We are holding the tension between our need for intimacy and our need for individuality while in relationships. Of course, we embrace both when we are with others, talking with others, working with others, playing with others. But, quite honestly, that is a challenging project. No wonder most of the emails I received were stories of broken relationships. Combining the expectations of happily ever after and the singleness of fulfillment is too much. People cannot sustain it.

We need a reassessment of relationships in the second half of life. This includes both broadening and deepening our connection with one another. The broadening involves a reassessment of our expectations of one another. We cannot be all things to one another. Therefore, we need a larger community with greater variety. For example, I've witnessed a renewed energy in my mother, who suddenly uprooted herself from her neighborhood of thirty-five years to relocate at the age of 79. My initial reaction centered around concern that she was abandoning a place that supported her. But I was wrong. That neighborhood had become narrow and small. She sought something larger. Today she is engaged in multiple activities with new friends and greater variety. It has given her life and strength. Now 88, she has a community.

---

[9] Schmidt, "Individuation: finding oneself in analysis" *Journal of Analytical Psychology,* 2005, vol 5, 612.

Yet we also need opportunities to go deeper in our connections with others and ourselves. For decades, Jane had an abundance of friends. She worked in health care her whole life, respected by her peers, and appreciated by her neighbors. Yet she needed something more. "I certainly didn't need or want more friends. I had plenty," she told me. "But I was hungry for something more in terms of meaning." So, on a suggestion from a friend in her synagogue, she enrolled in a spiritual companionship program where she could dive deeper into her faith. But that's not what happened. Instead, the program threw her upside down, and she found her beliefs challenged. For two years, she struggled with the readings, the lectures, and the projects. How did she do? "I loved it. I loved every single bit of the discussions, the debates. It pushed me in ways I never imagined. I now have more engaged conversations with people in my synagogue and my friends in the neighborhood."

I've come to embrace that quote from Martin Schmidt. "Becoming oneself demands perpetual risk-taking and sacrifice within relationships." It's been true in my marriage, my career, my friendships. The more I lean into others, the more I grow as an individual. That's Weird Wisdom.

Chapter 7

Destiny

I have always believed, and I still believe, that whatever good or bad fortune may come our way we can always give it meaning and transform it into something of value.

— *Hermann Hesse, Siddhartha*

For most of my life, I have battled between two callings. I heard the voice of practicality, application, and productivity whispering in one ear. In the other ear I heard the voice of wonder, mystery, and the sacred. In between, a trickster danced to keep the two separated, like twin brothers destined to fight. Living between these two callings suggests a form of schizophrenia, which may not be far from the truth. Though I do not use that word in its clinical understanding, I suggest we all have an ecosystem of voices calling to us regularly.

As we journey through the midpoint of life and begin to examine who we are and what we truly value, we inevitably realize our limitations. This comes in various forms. The actor Dustin Hoffman once articulated it this way in a *60 Minutes* interview. "I realize I can't double my age anymore. When I was 30, I could imagine 60. When I was 40, I could still imagine 80, but now I'm in my 50s. I can't double that anymore." Hoffman found a creative way of articulating something we all face in the second half of life, namely that time has become our most important commodity.

Facing the limits of our time on earth can make late-modern humans engage in some peculiar behaviors. We purchase boats or sports cars. We obsess with youth culture to reclaim youthful energy. Some choose to alter their physical appearance through surgery, injections, or maybe just the addition of body piercings or tattoos. It's as if we believe we can stop or slow down the process of aging. In the 17th century, Ponce de Leon was supposed to have searched Florida for a fantasy sometimes called the fountain of youth. We're still looking for it, and though Florida is a hotbed of these pursuits, the locations vary widely.

In this chapter, I want to toss in a bit of weirdness and suggest that, facing the time limits of life, we might consider an alternative to speedboats and Botox. That alternative centers on our destiny, a calling to stand apart from others, be unique, maybe a little weird.

Destiny has less to do with finality and more to do with identity. We could call upon the wisdom of Darth Vader when he calls out to Luke Skywalker in the *Star Wars* film mythology, "It is your destiny." Words of any father to a son, translated as, "Luke, don't go off on your own, just come back home to the family business, and be just like me." Many a young person echoes Luke's "Noooooo!" To be clear, it's not that going home and following in our parents' footsteps does not have value, but it's the parental foot imprinted on the child to "do it my way" that sends us running. It's the denial of the individual's growth to go out on their own, separate, and become their own person…weirdness and all.

Destiny is a word with roots in the Latin *destinare*, implying that we are "of the stars."[1] When we consider some of the scientific theories of a cosmic Big Bang resulting in the stuff of the stars bursting into all aspects of life throughout the universe, including the carbon within our bodies … it makes sense. We are stardust. To be of the stars conjures up the idea of aspiration. We are summoned to be of the stars and to aspire to a life filled with fullness, brightness, and clarity of purpose. But destiny also means "to stand out, or stand apart, to be unique."[2] In the time we have left on earth, we are wise to use that time to manifest a unique contribution to the world and shape a meaningful life. As I mentioned

---

[1] Meade, *Fate and Destiny: The Two Agreements of the Soul*, 3.
[2] Ayto, *Dictionary of Word Origins*, 166.

earlier, the word "weird" is related to the German *werden* meaning "to become or to grow."[3] So you can see the connection between destiny and weirdness.

Our destiny is to embrace our weirdness, unique nature, and character quality. Our destiny is the way the Creator weaves and shapes our life. Our inner and outer weirdness is also our divine connection. This destiny of life is to awaken to how the sacred speaks to us and through us. This voice of the sacred beckons us to live out our personality and the inner weirdness that makes us each a unique spark of creation.[4]

We need a weird ancient story of destiny to find our way around this topic. The Hebrew Bible story of Jonah is among my favorites. It's the tale of a person not so much in search of his personal destiny as being pursued by destiny. If you are not familiar with the whole story, I suggest pulling out a Bible and reading it now. But I'll provide a summary here. Several key personalities, including Jonah, the captain and the ship's crew, a rather large fish, the people of Nineveh, and one persistent deity, dominate this story.

In chapter 1, God directs Jonah to go to Nineveh, described as a great city filled with a healthy dose of wickedness. Jonah calculates that he knows better or has no interest in this call. He boards a ship headed in the opposite direction for Tarshish, possibly located on the coast of Spain. The sailors of the boat become concerned as a great storm brews. While all this is going on, Jonah is below deck, where the captain finds him taking a nap. Through a series of ancient practices, the equivalent of drawing straws, we learn that the cause of the storm is none other than Jonah himself. The sailors debate and Jonah soon volunteers to be thrown into the sea, which immediately causes the wind to cease. Next, God appoints a great big fish. Somewhere along the line, this got

---

[3] Meade, *Fate and Destiny: The Two Agreements of the Soul*, 6.
[4] ibid.

translated into a whale. It's inside the belly of this giant sea monster that Jonah spends three nights and three days. Hmmm, I see a pattern.

Chapter 2 consists of Jonah singing a long lament inside the belly of the great fish. His song is not a plea for help; it's a song of gratitude for his deliverance, which is a bit surprising because that hasn't happened yet. But we'll explore that later. The chapter concludes with the fish puking Jonah up onto the beach. You may suspect that I've manufactured that line, but it's there in just about every translation. Vomited is the accurate translation, though a few translators have tried to tame it with cough up, spat, threw up, spewed. I think you get the idea.

Chapter 3: After showering, Jonah yields to the instructions to go to Ninevah, circumnavigate it for three days, and speak wisdom to the people so that they might amend their wicked ways. His words are heeded, and the people, including the king, genuinely express remorse and turn their lives around. Even God is taken aback by this turnaround and chooses to suspend judgment. It's another one of those curious moments in the Bible, often overlooked, when human actions force a different outcome. Yes, human beings surprise God, and this deity has a change of mind.

In chapter 4, Jonah is a bit recalcitrant and throws a temper tantrum. He is still hoping to see some heads roll. Instead, Jonah confirms his suspicions all along, namely that this God is gracious and merciful, slow to anger, and abounding in steadfast love. The story concludes with a series of lessons involving plants, worms, and the sun, and all of it is another opportunity for Jonah to pout and for God to confirm his graciousness and steadfast love.

Dennis Dewey, one of the founders of oral Biblical Storytelling, once commented that he thought this might have been initially a kind of children's fairy tale. He then performed it, word for word, and when he came to the part where Jonah is "spewed" back onto dry land, I could imagine a host of 6-year-olds laughing uproariously. Dewey may be on to something because human history is filled with fairy tales that entertain and enlighten. Just ask the Brothers Grimm or Disney. I suspect the Jonah tale became a favorite among villages of families and people of all ages. Like any great story, it has something for everyone, a message on many levels.

Jonah hears a calling through a divine voice with a clear directive to live out his destiny as a prophet and speak to the wickedness of the people of Nineveh.[5] But his calling seems to originate before the divine revelation that he hears, in that Jonah's given name, from the Hebrew *yonah*, means a dove, suggesting that he was to embody the dove at an early age, and perhaps before his birth. The dove is a symbol often associated with peace, and in the Christian narratives, symbolizes the Holy Spirit. Yet, Jonah's name can also mean "one who vexes" like a mischievous troublemaker. Is Jonah bearing these two meanings to his name? Are peace and mischief-maker among the dominant voices in the ecosystem of his being? Perhaps Jonah's destiny is to work out this multiple calling. He's both in pursuit of and fleeing from his destiny. Just as we spend our lives heeding a diversity of voices.

Jonah is called to a challenging task. Speaking to the people of Nineveh is fraught with many dangers as this city of the Assyrian empire was known for its brutality, particularly against its enemies, including Jonah's people. No wonder he wants to head in the opposite direction, out to sea and holiday on the Mediterranean coast of Spain. Who among us, when given a choice, would not choose the easy path, the safe path, the path of happiness? Who needs this challenge to face the demons around us or within us? While serving in a college dorm as a resident advisor, I encountered a particularly challenging meeting in our hall. The Head Resident called the meeting, and it involved a poor decision I had made. In preparation for the meeting, she indicated that if I didn't want to attend, I could take a pass. I took the offer and

---

[5] Yee, Page & Coomer *The Old Testament and Apocrypha: Fortress Commentary on the Bible*, 861-869.

ran off to an overnight at a friend's house. When I returned, one of my roommates told me the meeting went well, "But you know Jim, you should have been there for it. That didn't look good." I didn't say anything, but inside I knew he was right. I opted for the coast of Spain rather than face the challenge in Nineveh.

Jonah's choice to run from his destiny is similar to many story motifs in which the protagonists flee from the call. The call to adventure is met with fear that needs overcoming. Second thoughts or even deep personal doubts about whether they are up to the challenge emerge. The problem they face may seem too much to handle and the comfort of a home far more attractive than the perilous road ahead. This would also be our response, and so we read Jonah's reluctance as our reluctance.

I recall the scene in J.R.R. Tolkien's *Lord of the Rings* epic, when Frodo, the young Hobbit who bears the responsibility of delivering the One Ring to its final destruction and end the madness that surrounds all Middle Earth, says to the wizard Gandalf, "I wish it need not have happened in my time." "So do I," said Gandalf, "and so do all who live to see such times. But that is not for them to decide. All we have to decide is what to do with the time that is given us."[6]

Once aboard the boat that will take Jonah far away from his problems, well, his issues follow him. Funny how that happens to us. Jonah is fleeing more than just a directive. He is fleeing his very essence, running from the very core of his being. Like it or not, Jonah's destiny is to be a prophet, to speak something significant to Nineveh. It is indeed his destiny that he flees. The further he runs from it, the greater the response. In this case, a mighty storm arises, and Jonah knows it's a storm meant for him. He's discovered below deck and sleeping. One wonders at this point in the parable if Jonah is dreaming. Is this storm an internal or an external storm unpredicted by the Weather Channel? Maybe it's both.

---

[6] JRR Tolkien, *The Fellowship of the Ring*, 64.

The solution proposed by Jonah and his shipmates is a deep dive into the tumultuous waters of the sea. The storm is calmed, and Jonah, rather than drowning, is swallowed by a great fish, where he remains three days and three nights. Now, as I've mentioned previously in this book but want to emphasize again, let's not take this literally and enter into a conversation about how it might be possible for a human being to survive inside the digestive system of a large fish with the possibility of some pocket of oxygen. Stop it. These stories are metaphorical tales that tell a more profound truth. Jonah is underwater, inside a fish for three days and three nights. These are all clues of what depth psychologists and modern theologians would define as images intended to suggest entering into the unconscious or a deep search into one's soul or a dark night of the soul. Jonah has a soul-searching experience with his identity, his calling in life, and yes, his destiny.

Suzanne Cremen relates the story of Lynn, a woman at midlife, reevaluating her career and her overall purpose in life. The months preceding this event described below were fraught with emotional and relational turmoil. Lynn had a background in environmental work with degrees in science, education, and psychology. For several months, shelived alone on a boat, working to stop the cruel business of shark finning. All this set the stage for this uncanny "belly of the whale" experience.

> One night I heard this thumping against the boat. I thought, what's the deal with that? The fishers had thrown a finned shark onto the deck of the boat.
> Now, sharks are one of my big symbols of fear because I saw a guy get bit by one when I was little. So, I knew this was a direct threat to me about what I was doing.
> I got disoriented on the boat in the middle of the night, hit my head on a winch, and knocked myself out. When I woke up, I was lying face-to-face with this dead, finned shark. For me, it was coming face to face with my greatest fears.

> And my greatest fears, of course, were not so much the shark, but what I was going to do with the rest of my life.
>
> The experience was so sobering and so instantly maturing to me that it just put my life into perspective. It doesn't mean I figured everything out at that moment because I didn't. It's a process. But it changed my life at that moment.[7]

Not many have such a dramatic encounter, but we do know moments of being in the belly of the whale. These are the periods of life that cause us to question our priorities, as was the case with the gentleman I described in Chapter 4, who heard a voice asking him to "remember your family" so that his career did not dominate his life. This auditory encounter spared him a more dramatic moment later in life. An even less dramatic but no less significant moment happened to Brian, a friend of mine.

Brian had been serving as a public-school teacher for about twenty years. He found the work enjoyable and personally rewarding as he mentored high school students through arduous algebra, geometry, and calculus studies. Along the way, he acquired a master's degree and the accompanying salary increase. But in his late 40s, he hit a flat spot. Work became routine, and he tired of the personnel politics that invariably occur in organizations. This period lasted for several years until one summer when a friend offered his fishing cabin in Maine. Brian talked it over with his wife, and they agreed he'd spend the summer in this rustic cabin in the woods. The summer came and went, but something had shifted when Brian returned to his classroom that fall. "I honestly don't know what happened," he said. "Maybe it was the simplicity of living without indoor plumbing and the Internet. The experience kind of served as a reset for me."

---

[7] Cremen, S.N. "Vocation as *psyche's* call: a depth psychological perspective on the emergence of calling through symptoms at midlife." *Int J Educ Vocat Guidance* **19**, 41–61.

It's hard to know what happened precisely, but Brian continues as a math teacher. As he nears his retirement age, he's looking at options that emphasize his appreciation for simplicity. He imagines hiking portions of the Appalachian Trail, returning to that cabin in Maine, or finding a place in the woods like Thoreau. Brain realized his calling was indeed that of a math teacher, but his melancholia called out to him as he entered the second half of life. That led him to reconnect with nature and simplicity that served as a reset for his vocation.

Jonah comes to himself inside the belly of the whale. We don't exactly know what happened to him, but one thing is unique to this part of the story. Typically, in ancient myths, parables, and fairy tales, the protagonist in the story has an encounter with a monster or beast or another opponent and defeats his adversary. But this is a story in which our hero yields to the great fish under the sea. He is swallowed and carried on a three-night journey from west to east. Our hero goes into the darkness symbolizing a death-like experience. In that surrender, he rediscovers his calling and yields to the call of his destiny.[8]

Yielding is a central task in midlife. Hopefully, we have built up a sufficient degree of confidence in ourselves through school, work, military service, family, so that to yield to our destinies is less confusing, less terrifying. But those external foundations get us only so far. We may look around and say to ourselves, how did I get here, or wonder is this it? Many a man or woman have received the long-sought-after promotion, finally won the gold tournament, or been awarded the public recognition they long sought, only to find themselves a week or so later in a gloomy mood. For some, the mood lasts weeks, months, or more, and may turn into a form of depression. "I thought I was supposed to chase the golden ring," we say to ourselves. "But now that I have it, why am I here? It doesn't seem as satisfying as I thought it would be."

---

[8] Henderson in Jung, *Man and his Symbols*, 120.

As I've said earlier in this book, we should pursue those goals in the first half of life. That was our calling, but now having achieved it, or close enough, it's time for a new call. We wonder what our destiny is now. The answer is often found by letting forces shape us from a deeper level. A big part of yielding is a healthy dose of forgiveness. As we've made our way to this point, we've made decisions, prioritized certain aspects of ourselves. We've likely neglected people and parts of ourselves in making those choices.

It's important to remember that a degree of grace is a central aspect of our moving through these years. So many people, though not enough, reach a realization as the years go by that the regrets, mistakes, and losses we've had need to be released. "It's just too much work to cling to all that old crap," one 63-year-old said to me.

Jonah emerges from the whale still intact though significantly changed. He hears the call again and, this time, follows through with his journey. He confronts the Ninevites, and to his and God's surprise, the people turn their lives around. What about Jonah's speech makes the people respond so dramatically? Sure, we could dismiss it as just another biblical formula of the prophet having a gift. But I suspect it's something more significant. Jonah has been to the belly of the beast. He has been cast overboard and spewed upon the shore. In other words, Jonah has faced some struggles. We don't know the details, but it's clear that in his surrender to the depths of the ocean and all that it signifies, Jonah has undergone a kind of suffering. His time in the belly has inflicted a sort of collision with deep and powerful forces. Nevertheless, Jonah now has integrity and speaks as one with authority out of a lived experience with the divine, depths, and his calling and destiny.

In short, we could say that Jonah's words to the Ninevites carry with them the weight of a man who has been to hell and back. But, like a woman I knew who had years of sobriety and participation with Alcoholics Anonymous, when she stood before the weekly meeting of AA that occurred in a church basement and spoke, everyone listened.

They knew her words had the power of redeemed suffering. So likewise, Jonah's words resonate with the people of Nineveh because he has been in the steep of life. They hear his words and repent. Even God is surprised.

Although the average churchgoer may not be aware, there are several moments in the Hebrew scriptures when human actions impact God to such a degree that Yahweh changes the plan. Instead of destruction, God chooses grace. A gracious God disturbs Jonah, slow to anger and abounding in steadfast love and willing to amend the planned demolition.

The epic concludes with an almost Job-like dialogue where Jonah seemingly reverts to his immature attitude at the beginning of our story. God attempts to provide insight into the prophet about the ways of grace and redemption. The back and forth between Jonah and God continues. And perhaps that is the crucial lesson for our purposes. Like Jonah, we continue to be engaged in this ongoing conversation. Our destiny is not to a particular place or career. It's an embrace of an ongoing dialogue. We are constantly and consistently summoned to an adventure of which we cannot see the ending. Along the way, we resist, experience storms both external and internal, and invariably end up in the belly of a beast. We emerge strengthened and renewed, only to face new challenges and discover new learnings.

Our destiny is not to a particular role such as parent, firefighter, or nurse. Rather it is a call to engage in a dialogue where we ask the question, "What am I called to serve?" Thus, our call is to ask the question and engage in a conversational relationship with the world. We find our destiny in the ongoing dialogue where adversaries are without and within.

The second half of life presents us with a rich possibility for spiritual enlargement. After all, we have been through a lot in these many decades, and we are still around. We've learned a great deal, and now, in midlife, we have the chance to ask deeper questions.

What have I learned?
What wounds still burden me, and how can they contribute to my and others' healing?
What lessons of life and history do I know now?
Since I've been given a choice, how will I act now to further the life of others?
If God is indeed gracious, as Jonah learned, what difference does that make in my life?

The poet Mary Oliver captures this well in her poem "Wild Geese:"[9]

> You do not have to be good.
> You do not have to walk on your knees
> For a hundred miles through the desert, repenting.
> You only have to let the soft animal of your body
> love what it loves.
> Tell me about despair, yours, and I will tell you mine.
> Meanwhile the world goes on.
> Meanwhile the sun and the clear pebbles of the rain
> are moving across the landscapes,
> over the prairies and the deep trees,
> the mountains and the rivers.
> Meanwhile the wild geese, high in the clean blue air,
> are heading home again.
> Whoever you are, no matter how lonely,
> the world offers itself to your imagination,
> calls to you like the wild geese, harsh and exciting
> over and over announcing your place
> in the family of things.

---

[9] Oliver, *Devotions*, 347.

Epilogue

Dreams as Windows into Weird Wisdom

I know of no better way to explore the inner landscape and discover the weird wisdom we all seek than through dreams. While you may choose to work with a psychologist, spiritual director, or a dream group, the options for delving deeper into the source of weird wisdom are many. This chapter attempts to describe several different approaches in this area. Think of it as a kind of application of all that I have written so far.

In the Hebrew Bible, the amazing, confounding, and delightful book of Job includes a curious character named Elihu. He arrives on the scene after many of Job's friends have offered countless explanations for why Job is suffering. During the dialogue between Job and Elihu, Job expresses his disgust with God, and wonders, essentially, "What good is this God anyway, and why do we even need God?" (My paraphrase.) In Chapter 33, Elihu delivers a speech that contains this often-overlooked insight.[1]

> "But let me tell you, Job, you're wrong, dead wrong!
>   God is far greater than any human.
> So how dare you haul him into court,
>   and then complain that he won't answer your charges?
> God always answers, one way or another,
>   even when people don't recognize his presence.

---

[1] Thanks to my colleague, Dr. Sheri Kling, for bringing this Scripture reference to my attention. Sheri presented to the Haden Institute years ago using this passage from Job.

> In a dream, for instance, a vision at night,
>> when men and women are deep in sleep,
>> fast asleep in their beds—
> God opens their ears
>> and impresses them with warnings
> To turn them back from something bad they're planning,
>> from some reckless choice,
> And keep them from an early grave,
>> from the river of no return.
>> (Job 33:12-18, *The Message*)

How does God answer our prayers, laments, and pleas for guidance? Elihu offers one answer. "In a dream, for instance, a vision at night, when men and women are deep in sleep,

fast asleep in their beds." Lest you think I've just cherry-picked this verse, I'll note a few of the many dreams in the Scriptures. Jacob dreams of angels descending the ladder in Genesis 28:12. Joseph is asked to serve as the interpreter of Pharoah's dreams in Genesis 41:1-36. Solomon encounters God in a dream in 1 Kings 3:5-15. Joseph receives a visitation in a dream in Matthew 1:20-25. In Matthew 27:19, Pontius Pilate's wife reports a dream of great significance, which is ignored. There are numerous other references to dreams, night visions, and holy encounters while people slumber.

Beyond the Bible, we know of many nocturnal encounters throughout history. The mothers of St. Augustine, St. Bernard of Clairvaux, and St. Dominic all reported dreams that influenced their lives and their sons. Teresa of Ávila's *The Interior Castle* can also be explored through dream interpretation.[2]

---

[2] Authors who have explored these dreams include John Welch in *Spiritual Pilgrims: Carl Jung and Teresa of Avila* (New York: Paulist Press, 1982) and Marie-Louise von Franz in *Dreams* (New York: Shambala Publications, 1991)

Dreams are central to many of the world's religions, including Hinduism, Buddhism, and Islam. Some researchers speculate that dreams and death might be the twin towers shaping faith development in human beings dating back to the earliest hominids. The theory goes that as our ancestors witnessed the loss of family and tribal members to death, they met them in the dream world. This led to storytelling, followed by rituals around campfires, which may have included chanting, dancing, and reciting dreams that provided meaning and comfort to grieving people. The origins of spirituality and the religious impulse may be found in dreams. It's possible our ancestors gathered around the village campfire and told of seeing their loved ones who had passed away in their dreams. Over time, rituals that included song and dance were added to these gatherings. One can see glimpses of the beginning of religion in this process.[3]

Dreams are very much a part of the sacred journey of human beings. While the language is not always straightforward because the unconscious speaks in symbolic language, dreams are among the ways God speaks to people. Could dreams be a part of spiritual direction in a congregation or another context? Yes, they could, and many have conducted dream groups in various settings, including churches, synagogues, prisons, schools, hospitals, libraries and other community settings.

Before describing a method I use in dream exploration, let's pause to ask ourselves, what are dreams? In recent years, we've learned that dreams are closely related to the stage of sleep known as REM sleep, so named because of the rapid-eye movements one can witness while another is sleeping. Approximately four or five times in an average person's evening of sleep, we drop down into this state of the sleep cycle. In case you are wondering, most mammals dream. This electrochemical activity produces images and storylines. During this time, parts of our brains become highly active. The general conclusion of researchers is that the brain does not "turn off;" instead, it kicks into high gear.

---

[3] Bulkeley, *Dreaming in the World's Religions: A Comparative History*, 7-8.

The theories around dreams are varied, but most people now believe that dreams connect our conscious minds with our unconscious minds. This is at the heart of the research conducted in the late 19th and early 20th centuries by people like Sigmund Freud and Carl Jung. A lesser-known researcher named Fritz Perls came along and developed the concept that dreams are a pathway to integration. We grow, mature, and move toward wholeness as we integrate aspects of our unconscious into our conscious mind. Perls, Jung, and others further developed the idea that dreams serve many functions:

Dreams help our bodily health.
Dreams help us integrate strong emotions.
Dreams engage in creative problem-solving.
Dreams weave new learning into our memory.
Dreams are compensatory.

We could delve into detail regarding each of these, but for now, I merely want you to see this list. However, I call to your attention to that last function. This concept, developed by Jung and others, suggests that part of what's happening in dreams is a compensatory activity designed to lead each of us toward wholeness. This often involves a balancing of the tension of opposites.

An example may be someone who suffers from deep insecurity or inferiority and, in a dream, finds themselves as a superhero. Conversely, someone who holds a rather high opinion of themselves, or views themselves as superior to others, might have a dream bringing them down to earth. Marie-Louise von Franz tells the story of a case in which one of Carl Jung's patients articulated many "stupid prejudices and her stubborn resistance to reasoned argument." One evening the woman dreamed she had been invited to a social occasion. She was greeted warmly by the hostess, who announced that all her friends were present and expecting her. "The hostess then led her to a door and opened it, and the dreamer stepped into a cowshed." That's an example of a compensatory dream. The woman held prejudices against other people in her social circles, but the soul reached out to her through this dream, bringing her a reality check. Rather than being above the others, she steps in the manure. The dreamer can learn from that dream and integrate it into her day-to-day conscious attitude.[4]

In a similar vein, I once heard author and pastor John Maxwell remind a group of ministers, "You are never as good as those accolades you received, but you are also not as awful as your detractors describe you." To that end, I have in my desk drawer a collection of notes people have written to me over the years. There is a box full of compliments, and a separate one of letters that are more humbling. Whenever I'm feeling down, I'll pull out a few of the complimentary cards, but when I'm a bit full of myself, I'll reach for one of those more humbling notes.

Dreams very often seem nonsensical to our conscious mind. They include images of things that fly which in waking life do not, such as elephants; or outsized objects, such as blueberries the size of watermelons. The images seem mismatched, and incongruous.

Dreams can be just plain weird. But they are also filled with powerful symbolic imagery. For instance, a man I know left his career as a pharmaceutical company executive to become a science teacher in public schools. As he was making this transition, he dreamt of a baby surrounded by light floating over the threshold of a doorway he was to walk through. He came to view this dream as a symbol of stepping through the opening to a new chapter in life.

In my late 40s, I experienced a time of significant anxiety about my career as a minister. I described this dream in the introduction of this book. At the time, I doubted my role and worth. I had a dream in which I welcomed a bishop who was to preach at my church, which appeared as an old decaying stadium in crumbling ruins. After the worship service, a woman was introduced to me by the bishop. She looked at me

---

[4] Von Franz, *Dreams*, 4.

and said, "You have to rebuild your pastorate." In retrospect, the dream is relatively straightforward, but I remember not telling it to anyone for years because it contained some other disturbing elements which I have not revealed here. My dream informed me that I needed to begin the task of my second half of life: rebuilding an interior pastorate. This word, pastorate, originates from the Latin *pascere*, to lead to pasture, and the noun "pastor," a shepherd. Indeed, my calling began to shift from rebuilding that old stadium in ruins to building an interior pasture, a lush, fertile land, suitable for growing new crops.

Dreams are rich, mysterious, and sacred. They are also beneficial for the spiritual journey. What follows is a technique initially developed by Jeremy Taylor and Robert Haden. I learned about this form of group dream exploration while studying at the Haden Institute in Asheville, North Carolina, and the Monastery of Mount Carmel in Ontario, Canada. This process emphasizes what the originators call "Dream Projection." The basic concept centers around a dreamer telling their dream in a small group setting. Those hearers then imagine themselves dreaming the same dream and offering their commentary or projections. By doing so, the original dreamer hears a variety of imaginings, with which they can engage, modulate, or discard. It's critical to note that in this process, no one in the dream group, or dream circle as some call it, is to interpret the dream meaning for others. The role of the leader is critical in maintaining this boundary.

Jeremy Taylor's basic hints for a dream group are as follows:[5]

1. All dreams speak a universal language and come in the service of health and wholeness. There is no such thing as a "bad dream," only dreams that sometimes take a dramatically negative form to grab our attention.

---

[5] Taylor, Dream Network Journal.

2. Only the dreamer can confidently know their dream's meanings. This certainty usually comes in the form of a wordless "Aha!" of recognition. This "Aha" is a memory function and is the only reliable touchstone of dream work.
3. There is no such thing as a dream with only one meaning. Instead, all dreams and images are "overdetermined" and have multiple meanings and layers of significance.
4. No dreams come to tell you what you already know. Instead, all dreams break new ground and invite you to new understandings and insights.
5. When talking to others about their dreams, it is wise and polite to preface your remarks with "if it were my dream or in my dream." Always keep this commentary in the first person. This allows for delivering relatively challenging and confronting comments so that the dreamer may be able to hear and internalize them. It also can become the profound psychospiritual discipline of "walking a mile in your neighbor's moccasins."
6. All dream group participants should agree at the outset to maintain anonymity in all discussions of dream work. In the absence of any specific request for confidentiality, group members should be free to discuss their experiences openly outside the group, provided no other dreamer is identifiable in their stories. However, whenever any group member requests confidentiality, all members should agree to be bound automatically by such a request.[6]

How does a dream circle work?

You'll be surprised how many people will be curious about a dream circle. Announcing that you are starting a dream circle will generate

---

[6] Taylor, *The Wisdom of your Dreams*.

lots of interest. Before you know it, you'll have a half dozen curious dreamers ready to go. But, I suggest that the first step before all this is networking and inviting. Be a participant in a dream group yourself, ideally for several years. That apprenticeship is essential.

I began as a participant when I started my instruction at the Haden Institute and have continued participating in a group for several years. Learning by doing, listening, and watching is foundational. This apprentice model has served as the foundation for all learning throughout human history. It's still relevant today. If you are interested in being a participant in a monthly dream circle that meets online, contact me.

Once you have a group formed, the following outlines my practice.

Guidelines for Dream Groups

Working on dreams in a group can be a marvelously rich experience. It may be challenging to understand our dreams. Bringing them to a group of dream partners can help us see aspects of our dreams we might not have been able to perceive on our own. Meeting once a month tends to be the most common approach.

Below are some guidelines that are useful when working on dreams in groups, inspired by and loosely based on the work of Montague Ullman. These guidelines help to create a sacred environment where dreamers can feel safe sharing their dreams without fear that someone else will tell them what it means or otherwise violate the sanctity of their dream material.

Each group will need to have a leader that is experienced and trained in facilitating a dream group.

The leader organizes the meeting logistics. Most importantly, the leader will ensure that the following guidelines are observed. Groups may decide to have members take turns being the leader. It's essential that everyone agrees to confidentiality of all the material offered in the dream group.

The Process

1) Presentation of the dream

The leader will ask for a ready volunteer to share a dream. The dreamer then reads the dream aloud. Other participants may write the dream down while the dreamer is sharing. Alternatively, the dreamer may email copies of the dream to other group members. While the dream is being shared, no one speaks other than the dreamer. If other members have questions, they are not to raise them now.

2) Clarifying Questions

Once the dream has been shared, the leader will invite group members to ask clarifying questions. For example, if the dreamer mentions a person by name without explanation, group members may ask who that person is in the dreamer's life. If the dreamer shared that she felt in the dream the way she felt at her cousin's wedding, group members might ask how she felt at her cousin's wedding. Otherwise, group members may not ask about feelings. This step is to allow for clarification of the dream text only.

3) Group Responds

The group leader now asks the dreamer permission to give the dream to the group. If the dreamer concurs, group members are now free to share their associations about the dream as if it were their dream. At this time, each group member's contribution should begin with the statement, "In my dream .... " For example, the group member might say, "In my dream, the language professor is an old woman dressed in purple." Group members do not address their comments to the dreamer. In fact, typically the dreamer, while still in the room, has been asked to take a seat outside of the circle looking away from the group. If the group is meeting on Zoom, they may simply turn their video function off, while still listening to the dialogue.

Group members offer their retelling of all or parts of the dream as if it were their own. Everyone is encouraged to acknowledge that their associations are their projections of the material and should not hold back or censor themselves. Paradoxically, it is often the most personal associations that spark new insight on the dreamer's part.

4) Dreamer's response

When the group has finished associating with the dream, and the dreamer feels ready to proceed, the dream is given back to the dreamer. The dreamer is the only one who speaks during this stage. The dreamer can respond in any way they wish, including sharing reactions to people's associations, thoughts about the dream, or anything else. Silence is also a legitimate response on the part of anyone.

5) A Time for "Aha!"

My preference is to then ask everyone in the group to describe an "Aha!" This is a new learning or discovery they have made about themselves or about dream work in general. It's not unusual for people to reflect on some aspect that brought insight to their own lives.

6) Closing

In my experience, a closing ritual of some kind is appropriate. Some groups choose to end with silence, others have a song they sing together, or a closing verbal prayer is offered. One group I know opens each dream circle with a candle lighting, and then closes it with extinguishing the candle. Regardless of what you choose, some form of collective ritual is appropriate.

Exploring Dreams further

Another exercise has been devised by Robert Hoss.[7] It's often called the six magic questions.

Select an image from the dream, either your dream or one presented to the group in a dream circle.

---

[7] Hoss, *Dream Language*, 230-231.

Who or what are you in the dream? I am _____
What's my purpose? My purpose as ____ I _____
What do I like about X? As _____ I like _____
What do I dislike about X? As _____ I dislike _____
As X, what do you fear the most? As _____ I fear _____
As X, what do you desire the most? As _____, my greatest desire is _____
As _____ my message to the dreamer is_____

I'll give an example from one of my dreams. I am driving a go-kart through a northern Canadian town with a female friend. Of course, the dream is more involved than this, but I give you that summary to set the stage for working with an image. In this instance, I chose the go-kart as the image which stood out to me. I could have selected the road, the woman accompanying me, or other images. But I chose the go-kart because it was such an odd and peculiar image in the dream. I then worked through the questions as follows.

Who or what are you in the dream? I am the red go-kart.
What's my purpose? My purpose as the go-kart is to move efficiently through the town.
What do I like about X? As the go-kart, I like the energy and playfulness I possess.
What do I dislike about X? As the go-kart, I dislike how small I am in relation to all the other vehicles on the road. I feel vulnerable.
As X, what do you fear the most? As the go-kart, I fear getting knocked off the road.
As X, what do you desire the most? As the go-kart, my greatest desire is to zoom out of town with both people.
As the go-kart, my message to the dreamer is that we are on the road together. So let's protect one another and venture out of town to the open road.

Johnson's Inner Work Approach

Another approach, which is less group-focused and depends upon the individual dreamer, can be found in the excellent work of Robert A. Johnson. His book *Inner Work: Using Dreams and Active Imagination for Personal Growth* is the go-to guide in this field. Johnson utilizes a four-step approach:

1. Making associations
2. Connecting dream images to inner dynamics
3. Interpreting
4. Enacting rituals to make the dream concrete

Making associations involves a focused intention around the dream images. For instance, in my dream of the go-kart, I might write down words, or draw pictures that come to mind as I imagine that go-kart in the dream. For example, the following words came to mind: Go, proceed, move, cart, carry, child, play, small, Disneyland. That last one comes to mind because I recall a childhood experience of driving go-karts at Disneyland.

That leads to the second step of making the connections between dream images. I have made one connection with the Disneyland association; another might be with the word "go." I wonder if I'm going toward or away from something in my life. In the third step of interpretation, we assemble the information we've gathered from the first two steps and arrive at a meaning or understanding. In the fourth step it might be helpful to enact a ritual to help make the dream concrete.

Let's apply Johnson's approach to another dream. In the spring of 2021, after having spent a year in various stages of the COVID-19 pandemic, I had the following dream.

> *I am escaping from a prison or a hostage situation. Once out in the streets I see the village has square ancient homes and*

reminds me of a Mediterranean village. Making my way through the streets I'm followed by police. There is a crash of a vehicle. I'm not in it but the crash allows me to escape. Then there is a police officer with a science-fiction-like gun strapped to his torso. At first, I think he is coming for me but then realize he intends to help me. I enter one of the homes and go to the second floor. Someone I know lives here. I think it's my son. I have a thought go through my head that he is now living here alone. I go through the kitchen and enter a bedroom. The bed has been slept in as I see a comforter tossed aside. Then on the floor I see rings of miniature figures arranged in a circle, almost like a mandala. I surmise that some children have been here and arranged these figures for me to see. I am mesmerized by these miniature figures and the shape of the mandala. Suddenly, I'm aware that I am not alone in the room. I look up and see in the corner an animal. It's dark and at first, I think it's a bear but realize it's a big black dog. It comes toward me. I wonder if it's friendly or something to fear. As it comes close, I sense it wants to be petted which I do in a very loving manner. I seem to have a cracker or biscuit that I'm eating. It's shaped like a communion wafer. I break it in half and give it to the dog who eats it. I wake up.

This is a very rich and elaborate dream. I've spent a good deal of time with it over the years. And please, thank you, but no, I'm not interested in your interpretations of what this dream means. The important thing, which I've said before, but will repeat, is that the meaning of dreams can best be understood by the dreamer. Yes, skilled persons can offer counsel, but in my experience the best counsel has emerged from questions.

We could take any number of images and work with them, but I'm going to focus on the miniature figures arranged in a circular mandala. I'll work with this image and use Johnson's four-step approach.

When I first thought of the circle of figures, even while in the dream state I thought of a mandala. In the dream it's simply a bunch of toy figurines arranged in series of circles, but I realized it had the appearance of a mandala. You see these everywhere, but especially in the great religious traditions of the world from the Hopi people to the rose windows of European cathedrals to the sand painting of Tibetan Buddhist monks. A mandala is a circular geometric form comprised of symbols. They are often employed in the practice of meditation as a spiritual guidance tool or for designating a sacred or holy place.

Making Associations – Even within the dream I was making an association, but let's focus on the dream. What did I see in the dream? It's a circle of toy figures. The associations that come to mind include the words: round, home, circumference, mandala, Stonehenge, perfect, sphere, play, child, whole, holy, hole.

Connecting dream images to inner dynamics - This step involves connecting a specific dream image with an aspect of our inner selves. "We need to figure out what is going on inside ourselves that is represented by the situation in the dream," writes Johnson.[8] A clue to this is in reviewing the words associated with the image. Ask yourself which one "clicks," which one captures your interest. For me, I'm returning to the mandala. It was such a powerful association even within the dream itself. I began to wonder about a mandala, a tool for the spiritual journey, made of miniature toy figures left by children.

Interpretation is the third stage, and often comes much later than we wish. In fact, you may find that you have different or multiple interpretations. At this stage we ask questions like: What is the central, most important message that this dream is trying to communicate to me? What is it advising me to do? What is the overall meaning of the dream for my life? If I were to step back from just the image of the mandala alone, I would interpret this dream as calling me out of a place of captivity and into a new relationship with the sacred, and the sacred involves tiny childlike play, animals, and a relation to the holy

---

[8] Johnson, *Inner Work*, 65.

as captured in symbolism of the Communion host at the conclusion of the dream.

<u>Enacting a ritual to make the dream concrete</u>. It's one thing to think through the messages of dreams, but it's another thing to somehow make them concrete. What we want to do here is link the dream world with the waking world. Jungians would say: Link the unconscious to the conscious world. There are many ways to do this. Some people would paint a dream, others journal it, others could go purchase some miniature figurines and play with them. Candidly, I resisted this part of the process until I worked with my spiritual director on the dream during our monthly Zoom session. Toward the end of our conversation, she asked what I might do to make this dream real. For some reason, I blurted out, "Oh, I don't know, go make an altar in the woods." We wrapped up our time together and I went downstairs and made lunch. The phrase "make an altar in the woods" kept buzzing around in my brain. That afternoon, I walked into the woods behind our home, and for the next six hours, using my hands, I gathered small- and medium-sized granite rocks. I then cleared an area large enough for a person to lie down and made a circle of glacial stones. My own altar, circle, mandala.

Sigmund Freud once wrote that dreams are the royal road to the unconscious. Before Freud and Jung, there were the mystics, the shamans, and the medicine men and women who helped people incubate the imagery and symbols emerging from within. Indeed, the gods were the sources of health and healing. Yahweh spoke to the Hebrew people of old. Elihu was right. His often-ignored speech from the book of Job is an ancient reminder that God speaks to people through dreams. They are but one way to wisdom, however weird that may be.

Dream exploration is a way to explore the inner landscape and discover the weird wisdom we all seek, especially in the second half of life. We've spent a lifetime building up a portfolio of achievements, and experiences. But as we've made this turn toward the second half, something new is calling out for us to build. In my case it was a calling to rebuild my inner pastorate. Dreams have been immensely helpful sources of weird wisdom. Thanks to many who have guided me along the way, I am a bit weirder, and hopefully a bit wiser as well.

REFERENCES

Aizenstat, Stephen. Dreamtending (blog) https://dreamtending.com/blog/volume-xxxviii/

Ayto, John. *Dictionary of Word Origins: The Histories of More Than 8,000 English Words.* New York: Arcade Publishing, 2011.

Beebe, J., J. Cambray and T. B. Kirsch. "What Freudians Can Learn from Jung." *Psychoanalytic Psychology* 18:2 (2001): 213-242.

Bell, Rob. *What We Talk about When We Talk about God.* New York: HarperOne, 2014.

Brooks, David. "The Moral Bucket List." *New York Times*, April 12, 2015. https://www.nytimes.com/2015/04/12/opinion/sunday/david-brooks-the-moral-bucket-list.html

Bulkeley, Kelly. *An Introduction to the Psychology of Dreaming,* 2nd ed. Westport, CT: Praeger Publishing, 2017.

Bulkeley, Kelly. *Dreaming in the World's Religions: A Comparative History.* New York: New York University Press, 2008.

Crowley, Chris and Henry S. Lodge. *Younger Next Year: Live Strong, Fit, Sexy, and Smart—Until You're 80 and Beyond.* New York: Workman Publishing, 2019.

Dante Alighieri, *The Divine Comedy.* New York: Berkley, 2003.

Dodd, Celia. "All Grown Up." *Retirement Wisdom,* July 4, 2022, podcast. https://www.retirementwisdom.com/podcasts/all-grown-up-celia-dodd/

Chinen, Allan B. *Once Upon a Midlife: Classic Stories and Mythic Tales to Illuminate the Middle Years.* New York: Putnam Publishing Group, 1992.

Cremen, S. N. "Vocation as *Psyche's* Call: a Depth Psychological Perspective on the Emergence of Calling through Symptoms at Midlife." *International Journal for Education and Vocational Guidance* 19 (2019): 41-61.

Dorson, Richard M. *Folktales Told Around the World.* Chicago: University of Chicago Press, 1976.

Else, Liz, "Mary, Mary, Quite Contrary," *New Scientist,* November 3, 2001.

Fowler, James W. *Stages of Faith: The Psychology of Human Development and the Quest for Meaning.* San Francisco: Harper & Row, 1981.

Gafney, Wil. https://www.workingpreacher.org/commentaries/revised-common-lectionary/ordinary-20-2/commentary-on-proverbs-91-6

Gandhi, Mohandes. *An Autobiography: The Story of My Experiments with Truth.* New York: Dover Publications, 1983.

Gilligan, Carol. *In a Different Voice: Psychological Theory and Women's Development.* Cambridge: 1982.Harvard University Press,

Hatkoff, Craig. "From Arrogance and Failure to Helping Create the Tribeca Film Festival." https://www.fastcompany.com/3031100/from-arrogance-and-failure-to-helping-create-the-tribeca-film-festival

Hazelwood, James. *Everyday Spirituality: Discover a Life of Hope, Peace and Meaning* Wakefield, RI: Hazelwood Media, 2019.

Henderson, Joseph "Ancient Myths and Modern Man" in *Man and his Symbol*, edited by Carl Jung. New York: Double Day, 1976.

Hollis, James. *The Broken Mirror: Refracted Visions of Ourselves.* Asheville, NC: Chiron Publications, 2022.

Hollis, James. *Living an Examined Life: Wisdom for the Second Half of the Journey.* Asheville, NC: Chiron Publications, 2018.

Hollis, James. *The Middle Passage: From Misery to Meaning in Midlife.* Toronto: Inner City Books, 1993.

Hoss, Robert J. "The Psychology of Dreaming." https://www.dreamscience.org/wp-content/uploads/2019/02/Part-2-Psychology-of-Dreaming.pdf

Hoss, Robert J. *Dream Language: Self-Understanding Through Imagery and Color.* Ashland, OR: Innersource, 2005.

Johnson, Robert A. *Inner Work: Using Dreams and Active Imagination for Personal Growth.* San Francisco: HarperOne, 2009.

Jung, Carl. *The Collected Works of Carl Jung*, Translated by R.F.C. Hull. Bollingen Series XX. Princeton University Press.

Jung, Carl. "Psychology and Religion" in *Psychology and Religion: East and West.,"* Vol. 11 of *The Collected Works of C. G. Jung,* translated by R. F. C. Hull, edited by Herbert Read et al. Princeton: Princeton University Press, 1958

Jung, Carl. "The Psychology of the Transference" in *The Practice of Psychotherapy,"* Vol. 16 of *The Collected Works of C. G. Jung,* translated by R. F. C. Hull, edited by Herbert Read et al. Princeton: Princeton University Press, 1954.

C.G. Jung. *Selected Letters of C.G. Jung, 1909-1961.* Edited by Gerhard Adler. Princeton, NJ: Princeton University Press. 1984

Jung, Carl. *Two essays on analytical psychology.* London: Routledge & Kegan Paul. 1953.

Jung, Carl. *The Portable Jung.* Edited by Joseph Campbell. New York: Penguin Books, 1976.

Kierkegaard, Søren. *Kierkegaard's Journals and Notebooks: Volume 2, Journals EE-KK,* edited by Bruce H. Kirmmse et al. Princeton: Princeton University Press, 2015.

Lachman, Margie E. "Development in Midlife." *Annual Review of Psychology* 55 (2004): 305-331.

Lane, Belden C. *The Great Conversation: Nature and the Care of the Soul.* Oxford: Oxford University Press, 2019.

Levinson, Daniel J. et al. *The Seasons of a Man's Life.* New York: Alfred A. Kopf, 1978.

Lippert, Laura. "Women at Midlife: Implications for Theories of Women's Adult Development." *Journal of Counseling & Development*, 76 (Winter 1997):16-22.

Lockhart, Russell. "Speaking of Jung—Episode 16." *Speaking of Jung: Interviews with Jungian Analysts* (blog) April 16, 2016. https://speakingofjung.com/podcast/2016/4/16/episode-16-russ-lockhart

Main, Roderick. *Revelations of Chance: Synchronicity as Spiritual Experience*. Albany: State University of New York Press, 2007.

Mason, Nadya. "How to Spark Your Curiosity, Scientifically." https://www.youtube.com/watch?v=OMDVTZ-ycaY

Meade, Michael. *Fate and Destiny: The Two Agreements of the Soul*. rev. ed. Housatonic, MA: Green Fire Press, 2012.

Meyer, Marvin, Ed. *The Nag Hammadi Scriptures*. The International Edition. New York: Harper One, 2007

Newman, B. M. and P. R. Newman. *Development Through Life: A Psychosocial Approach*. 7th ed. Homewood, IL: Dorsey Press, 2018.

Oliver, Mary. *Devotions: The Selected Poems of Mary Oliver*. New York: Penguin Publishing, 2020.

Plato, *Dialogs of Plato* New York: Dover Publications, 2007.

Reps, Paul and Nyogen Senzaki, comps. *Zen Flesh, Zen Bones: A Collection of Zen and Pre-Zen Writings*. Rutland, VT: Charles E. Tuttle Company, 1957.

Rohr, Richard. *Immortal Diamond: The Search for Our True Self.* New York: Jossey-Bass, 2013.

Schmidt, Martin. "Individuation: Finding Oneself in Analysis—Taking Risks and Making Sacrifices." *Journal of Analytical Psychology* 50, vol. 5 (November 2005): 595-616.

Daryl Sharp Jungian Lexicon: A Primer of Terms and Concepts. https://www.psychceu.com/Jung/sharplexicon.html

Sinigaglia, Ornella. "A Brief History of Doubt." *Maize* (31 May 2021) https://www.maize.io/columns/a-brief-history-of/a-brief-history-of-doubt

Slee, Nicola ed. *The faith lives of women and girls: Qualitative research perspectives.* Routledge, 2013

Slee, Nicola. *Women's Faith Development: Patterns and Processes.* Burlington, VT: Ashgate Publishing, 2004.

Stimson, William R. "Montague Ullman's Dream Appreciation." *The Humanistic Psychologist* 41:2 (Apr-Jun 2013): 178-198.

Tacey, David. *The Post-Secular Sacred: Jung, Soul, and Meaning in an Age of Change.* New York: Routledge, 2019.

Taylor, Jeremy. *The Wisdom of Your Dreams: Using Dreams to Tap Into Your Unconscious and Transform Your Life.* New York: Tarcher Perigee, 2009.

Tolkien, J.R.R. *The Fellowship of the Ring.* Boston: Houghton Mifflin, 2001.

Valantasis, Richard. *The Gospel of Thomas.* New York: Routledge, 1997.

Vervaeke, John and Jonathan Pageau. "Curiosity and Wonder." *Rebel Wisdom*, streamed live on June 16, 2022. YouTube video, https://www.youtube.com/watch?v=mrdJJCKkwdI.

Von Franz, Marie-Louise. *Dreams.* New York: Shambala Publications, 1991.

Von Franz, Marie-Louise. "Individuation" in *Man and His Symbols,* edited by Carl Jung. New York: Doubleday, 1976.

Weber, Max. *From Max Weber: Essays in Sociology.* Translated and edited by H. H. Gerth and C. Wright Mills. New York: Oxford University Press, 1946.

Welch, John. *Spiritual Pilgrims: Carl Jung and Teresa of Ávila.* New York: Paulist Press, 1982 .

Weller, Francis. *The Wild Edge of Sorrow: Rituals of Renewal and the Sacred Work of Grief.* Berkeley, CA: North Atlantic Books, 2015.

Whyte, David. *Essentials*. Orcas Island, WA: Many Rivers Press, 2020.

Yee, Gale A., Hugh R. Page and Matthew J. M. Coomber, eds. *The Old Testament and Apocrypha.* Minneapolis: Fortress Press, 2014.

Zacharia, Paul. "The Surprisingly Early History of Christianity in India." *Smithsonian Magazine* (February 19, 2016) https://www.smithsonianmag.com/travel/how-christianity-came-to-india-kerala-180958117/

Websites

https://www.ted.com/talks/brene_brown_the_power_of_vulnerability?utm_campaign=tedspread&utm_medium=referral&utm_source=tedcomshare

https://news.harvard.edu/gazette/story/2017/04/over-nearly-80-years-harvard-study-has-been-showing-how-to-live-a-healthy-and-happy-life/

https://www.theatlantic.com/family/archive/2022/02/happiness-age-investment/622818/

https://warwick.ac.uk/newsandevents/pressreleases/researchers_find_that/

https://archive.nytimes.com/well.blogs.nytimes.com/2008/01/30/the-midlife-crisis-goes-global/

https://www.theatlantic.com/business/archive/2011/06/the-pursuit-of-happiness-what-the-founders-meant-and-didnt/240708/

https://www.archives.gov/founding-docs/virginia-declaration-of-rights

https://content.time.com/time/magazine/article/0,9171,2019628,00.html

https://pursuitofwonder.com/

https://www.soulhealfilm.com

https://www.pbs.org/wgbh/t/frontline/shows/religion/story/thomas.html

http://www.thresholdguidance.com/?page_id=254

https://dreamnetworkjournal.com/@jeremytaylor/

https://www.marquette.edu/maqom/Gospel%20of%20Thomas%20Lambdin.pd

ACKNOWLEDGEMENTS

This book is also the result of my work with numerous teachers, therapists, spiritual directors, pastors, and friends. I'm grateful to all of you. Saints and Sinners that you are. Much gratitude to John Carlson, Paul Evenson, Paul Fauske, Duke Fries, Paul Sanderson, John Romig Johnson, Brewster Beach, Jennie Isabel Shinn, Vaneta, Sigmar Schwarz, John Kuethe, Ann Ulanov, Don Green, and the Frank Bros.

The editor for this book, Janna Eversmeyer. Thank you for your attention to detail and your encouragement.

My education in Spiritual Direction at the Haden Institute & the Monastery at Mt. Carmel formed the backdrop of this book. Thank you for holding Christian Mysticism and the Depth Psychology of Carl Jung in a healthy tension.

This book is dedicated to my family. Lisa, Ben, Amanda, Asa, Nick, Carol, Art & Dan.

James Hazelwood is an author, spiritual director, pastor, photographer, touring cyclist and currently serves as Bishop of the New England Synod (ELCA Lutheran). He is a graduate of the Haden Institute & Mt. Carmel Monastery training program in Spiritual Direction. His spiritual direction is primarily with men seeking to navigate the quandaries of modern life. In addition to *Weird Wisdom for the Second Half of Life*, he is also the author of *Everyday Spirituality: Discover a Life of Hope, Peace and Meaning.*

He writes regularly at www.jameshazelwood.net

www.ingramcontent.com/pod-product-compliance
Lightning Source LLC
Chambersburg PA
CBHW071854070526
44583CB00016B/1689